EPIPHANIES
of *Nature*
& *Grace*

EPIPHANIES
of Nature
& Grace

Twelve Meditations from
a Life in Dialogue

Cyprian Consiglio

ORBIS ✪ BOOKS
Maryknoll, New York 10545

Founded in 1970, Orbis Books endeavors to publish works that enlighten the mind, nourish the spirit, and challenge the conscience. The publishing arm of the Maryknoll Fathers and Brothers, Orbis seeks to explore the global dimensions of the Christian faith and mission, to invite dialogue with diverse cultures and religious traditions, and to serve the cause of reconciliation and peace. The books published reflect the views of their authors and do not represent the official position of the Maryknoll Society. To learn more about Maryknoll and Orbis Books, please visit our website at www.orbisbooks.com.

Library of Congress Cataloging-in-Publication Data

Names: Consiglio, Cyprian author
Title: Epiphanies of nature and grace : twelve meditations from a life in dialogue / Cyprian Consiglio.
Description: Maryknoll, NY : Orbis Books, [2025] | Summary: "Meditations on Christian mysteries that draw on the author's monastic vocation and his life in dialogue between the spirituality of East and West"—Provided by publisher.
Identifiers: LCCN 2025005066 (print) | LCCN 2025005067 (ebook) ISBN 9781626986237 paperback | ISBN 9798888660782 epub
Subjects: LCSH: Camaldolese—Spiritual life | Monastic and religious life—Meditations | Epiphanies | Christianity and other religions | East and West
Classification: LCC BX3085 .C66 2025 (print) | LCC BX3085 (ebook) | DDC 255—dc23/eng/20250524
LC record available at https://lccn.loc.gov/2025005066
LC ebook record available at https://lccn.loc.gov/2025005067

Dedicated to the memory of Mark, Michael, and David,
brothers who couldn't make it to the end;
and to Dan Riley, OFM, a fellow pilgrim who made it,
but it's still hard to imagine the world, the Church,
or my life without him in it.

"There is a light that can overcome the darkness,
but there is no darkness that can overcome the light."

Beloved, we are God's children now;
what we will be has not yet been revealed.
What we do know is this:
when he is revealed, we will be like him,
for we will see him as he is.

1 John 3:2

I know that Great Person
of the sunlight splendor beyond the darkness.
Only in knowing that one do we go beyond death:
there is no other way to go.

Svetasvatara Upanishad, III.8

In our time, when day by day humankind is being drawn
closer together, and the ties between different peoples are
becoming stronger, the Church examines more closely
her relationship to non-Christian religions. In her task of
promoting unity and love among people, indeed among
nations, she considers above all what people have in common and what draws them to fellowship.

Nostra Aetate of Vatican II

Contents

Introduction

On a Life in Dialogue

There was something I noticed in the later writings of two authors I admire greatly, both of whom I had the great good fortune to meet before their passing. The first was Bede Griffiths, an English Benedictine monk who lived for thirty-eight years in India and was the third of three founders of the first major Christian ashram there, Shantivanam, where I sit as I write these words. The other was William Johnston, an Irish Jesuit who spent nearly fifty years living in Japan, a professor at Sophia University in Tokyo. Both of them were considered to be pioneers in the field of East-West dialogue, Griffiths mainly for his encounter with Hinduism and Johnston for his with Zen Buddhism, and they published many books between them about their speculations, discoveries, and re-articulations of the kerygma of Christianity through those lenses. But I am particularly thinking of Bede's *New Creation in Christ* and Johnston's *Mystical Theology* and *Arise My Love.* There did not seem to be a "compare and contrast" between Asian and European spirituality (a term I prefer to "East-West," which I will explain below) going on in their writings by their last years. Each spoke now from Asia, now from Europe, seamlessly, as if they were not two. There is just a perennial philosophy or, as Bede would call it, universal wisdom. (I ought to add the prolific giant in this ambit Raimundo Panikkar to this list as well, at a much higher academic level, who often quoted the ancients in Greek and Sanskrit in the same sentence.) I have gently challenged my friends who teach philosophy to be inspired by this approach. And I wonder aloud, "Is there ever going to come a day when undergraduate survey courses of the History of Philosophy in the Western world will be like this, and not teach only European philosophers, while maybe offering an elective on Asian philosophy, almost as an afterthought?" This combination is the world we live in, and the intellectual world we ought to broaden ourselves to.

I mention this to explain that I was fortunate to be able to study Western European and Asian mysticism and spirituality in parallel tracks from the first days of my monastic life. I had early on come under the sway of Fr. Bede as he visited our community in California on his way back to India, where he would die nine months later.

I belong to one of the smallest monastic congregations in the Catholic Church under the mantle of the Benedictine Confederation, the Camaldolese. We began as a reform movement within the monastic world of medieval Italy, inspired by the example of Saint Romuald of Ravenna. After a few years as a regular observance Benedictine monk, Romuald launched out on his own, putting himself under the tutelage of a hermit near Venice and ended up being revered as a spiritual master himself. He was consequently called upon by the ecclesial and imperial authorities (a personal friend of the young Emperor Otto III) to both reform and found monasteries and hermitages up and down the Italian peninsula. Some of his earliest disciples were also missionary martyrs in lands that were then hostile, Poland and Hungary. Thus our signature charism was established in the first moment, what we call the *triplex bonum*, the "threefold good": community, solitude, and this third good, which we really don't like to name. It's some kind of absolute availability, but it originally was missionary martyrdom. Fr. Bede had brought himself and his ashram community in India into the Camaldolese Congregation in 1983. As a matter of fact, our former Prior General once pointed to Fr. Bede Griffiths as a modern example of that third good, not that he had necessarily faced martyrdom, but because he had gone so far out of his comfort zone—an Oxford-educated Englishman living the last years of his life in the very austere lifestyle of an ashram in India—and for his well-known work in interreligious dialogue.

My liberal-minded and far-sighted prior at that time, seeing how deeply I had been moved by my encounter with Bede and his teaching, actually encouraged me in these parallel tracks. So while I was studying liturgy, monastic history, and the patristic writers of the earliest years of Christianity, I was putting myself through a self-tutorial on the history of Buddhism (I learned early on that monks are notorious autodidacts, and I fell easily, happily into that category). I also dove deeply into the writings of Bede Griffiths and his fiery French Benedictine peer and predecessor at Shantivanam, Henri Le Saux, who adopted the Sanskrit name Abhishiktananda, as well as all the source material they referred to, particularly the Upanishads. This broad and inclusive approach feels so normal and natural to me by now that I often have to remind myself that it is not so for most Christians, nor for other Catholic religious, even monks. When preaching and teaching for my own monastic community I could get away with a lot of references to these things. In my first years as a member of the community there were still other monks alive who were well enough steeped in that vocabulary to absorb it, and then after a while my community just got used to me too, perhaps with an occasional rolled eye. I slowly learned that in a normal environment, however, you have to explain some of the backstory of things like non-duality or the mysticism of the Sufis.

The reading and studying were not enough, however. Intellectual curiosity and spiritual hunger led me to spend ten years of my monastic life living away from my community engaged in an experimental life in which I lived part time in a hermitage in the woods near a town on the central coast of California and the rest of the time actively involved in interreligious dialogue through music, encounters, study, immersion and, most of all, relationships. This work led me to travel literally all over the world, besides America and Europe, much time in Southeast Asia and Australia, and finally to Lebanon, Syria, and Israel. I went wherever I was invited, offering what I could in terms of music or teaching and absorbing all I could from the new persons and environments in which I was immersed. After another ten years living back with my community serving as prior, I was asked to take on the role of Secretary General for Monastic Interreligious Dialogue for the Benedictine Confederation, so now what I had wanted to return to by aspiration I have been called to do by mandate.

Why I prefer not to use the phrase "East/West" is because it is a very Eurocentric concept, and if there is anything I have been pursuing in Christianity, it is its breaking out of its Eurocentric container to really becoming a world church, particularly my own communion Catholicism. And I always try to specify "Western European" because that is what is in my DNA. And so for the most part the interreligious dialogue happening in this book is taking place between Western European Christianity and Asian mysticism and philosophy.

Hence, the subtitle of this collection, "Twelve Meditations

from a Life in Dialogue." However, "dialogue" means more
to me than simply comparative religion and interreligious
dialogue. It was only looking back that I realized how deeply
Fr. Bede had more broadly influenced my understanding of a
theology of the Word, meaning that wherever we see Beauty,
Truth, and Goodness manifesting, those transcendentals of
the Greek philosophers, we are seeing a glimpse of who we
would call the Second Person of the Trinity. *Wherever* we
see them. Along with that, I consider myself to be totally a
child of Vatican II, the council that opened the windows of
my communion, the Catholic Church, not only to dialogue
with the world, but to being a world church instead of just
a European one. This was nowhere more evident than in the
council's groundbreaking document called *Nostra Aetate,* the
"Declaration on the Relation of the Church to Non-Christian
Religions," which was nothing short of an about-face from
the Counter-Reformation stance that the Church had held
for centuries. And could not all this be part of the new evangelization that the last three popes called for, "new ardor, new
methods, and new expressions"?

Let me add another dialogue in which I find myself engaged. An anecdote to illustrate it: I especially loved Pope
Benedict XVI's book *Jesus of Nazareth* and had actually read
a lot of his writing well before he was pope. My musical
collaborator John Pennington and I were doing a concert
in Colorado for a center called Boulder Integral, a spiritual
center in the school of the American writer Ken Wilber's
Integral Theory, some years back, featuring the songs that
we have written based on various spiritual traditions. To
"represent" Christianity we did a piece I wrote called "Unless
a Grain of Wheat," because I think it contains some of the
universal wisdom for the spiritual life that Christianity has
to offer. I introduce it by quoting Pope Benedict saying that

the phrase *Unless a grain of wheat shall fall into the ground and die it remains a single grain, but if it dies it will yield a rich harvest,* from the Gospel of John,[1] sums up all Jesus' parables. The next day, as we were driving away from Boulder, John said to me rather hesitatingly, "You quote Pope Benedict a lot." "Yes," I said. "People don't like him," he rejoined. And I said, "That's exactly why I quote him. If we are going to be in dialogue it can't only be with people we agree with, and I need to be in dialogue with my own tradition."

This, however, is not always or simply a cunning device. This also just comes naturally to me. You will see in the meditation titled "A Body You Have Prepared for Me," for example, I unwittingly found Sam Keen and Wendell Berry agreeing with John Paul II and Christopher West. Nothing delights me more.

And so, the meditations contained here will be sprinkled with a little of all that.

A note about the word "meditation" in the subtitle. If I may generalize a little bit, broadly speaking there is a European understanding of that word and an Asian one, which are almost diametrically opposed. For most Western Christians, to "meditate" means to expand on a thought. In the ancient practice of *lectio divina* (sacred reading), the second of four stages of the practice is called *meditatio*. It means "to ruminate"; the ancients compared it to what a cow does with her cud—chew it up, partially swallow it, spit it up again and chew some more, until you get all the savor out of it. Actually, "ruminating" is considered a negative thing in psychology, something you want to stop doing because it's usually associated with dark obsessive thoughts. This is a marvelous practice, however, if done in the right context, expanding

---

[1] Jn 12:24.

and letting the imagination run free . . . but only for a time.

The Asian sense of the word "meditate" goes the other way, bringing the mind to one-pointedness, what India refers to with the Sanskrit word *ekāgratā*, away from all the wandering thoughts. This would be the understanding of meditation in both the Buddhist tradition and the practice of yoga—"stilling the thought waves of the mind." This is where paying attention to the body, the breath, and a simple prayer word or mantra come in. Interestingly enough, though you rarely hear it spoken about in this way, in my understanding this is what is called for in the fourth stage of *lectio divina*, which that tradition calls *contemplatio*, contemplation. I have practiced and made attempts to teach and write about meditation in what I am calling the Asian understanding for many years. This, however, is a collection of meditations in the *lectio* sense. And yet you will find in here some of my "meditations about meditation" (particularly "The Still Small Voice") and the vital importance of the contemplative dimension for the renewal of our minds and the evolution of our consciousness.

As I mentioned, I served for ten years as the superior (prior) of our community in California, and I considered preaching and teaching to be one of the main tasks in that role. Many of the meditations in this collection started out as short homilies for the community, or else they contain bits and pieces from the research done for my regular Chapter conferences, which here in this context I have been able to ruminate on a little bit more, and let my thoughts run a little freer.

Now a word on the main title of this collection. I must honestly admit, one day when someone asked me if I had a title for the new book, I actually did not, but I found myself spontaneously saying, "Epiphanies of Nature and Grace," not even knowing what it meant. It just came to me. It was only in afterthought that I realized that it was connected with an aphorism of Saint Thomas Aquinas that is absolutely foundational for my optimism about the human spirit: *Gratia non tollit naturam sed perfecit*—"Grace does not destroy nature but perfects it." Whatever is created, including especially the glory of the human person in the image of God, is already good. Divine grace does not need to cover over us and destroy all that to start all over again—our music, our art, the wonders of Nature, intelligence and creativity, our loves and our desires. It works with it; it brings it to its fruition. I once heard Huston Smith, the great scholar of World Religions, teach that the Judeo-Christian Scriptures are the only tradition that starts with that kind of positivity about creation. The whole canon of Scripture begins, in the Book of Genesis, with the Divine One intentionally creating the world and all its creatures, and at the height of that work the human person, and then saying, *God saw everything he had made, and indeed, it was very good.*[2]

By trade I still think of myself as a singer-songwriter as much as anything. Probably the most powerful retreat I ever made was in Snowmass, Colorado, a guest of the Cistercian monks there, who had a beautiful cabin 9,000 feet up in the Rocky Mountains, about four miles up a steep rock-strewn dirt road from the monastery. (They even loaned me an old four-by-four truck to make the journey.) I was in blissful solitude for ten days. The final day of my retreat I had the urge to write a song. I had been meditating all week on a verse from the prophet Hosea, when God says, in my paraphrase of it, "I will lead you into the desert with me, and tenderly speak to your heart."[3] That became the kernel for the new

---

[2] Gen 1:31.
[3] Cf. Hos 2:14.

song, and I was humming a possible refrain to myself for some hours before I went to sleep that night. But then I awoke suddenly at about 1:30 a.m. (that has historically been my bewitching hour) and was inspired to write the rest. By dawn I had a completed lyric.

In the third refrain I ask myself, "What did you go out to the desert to see? Did anything speak to your heart?" And my response to that lyric was:

> I saw mountains in summer still covered with
>   snow;
> I heard coyote howl for no reason I know.
> A thunderstorm passed at my level of sight,
> and dawn slipped in early through some crack in
>   the night.
> A bee seemed to buzz flying straight through my
>   head,
> and a bird sang vespers for me in my stead.
> Words flew on wings in the cool evening air,
> and I spoke to you often as if you were there.

I was somewhat disappointed by how it turned out. I guess I had been hoping to write something "holier" or more "spiritual." Then on second thought I realized what I had written were all things I had actually seen, experienced, epiphanies, if you will, that had moved me to silence, to awe, nearly to tears, manifestations of the Divine that made me understand and accept my place in the Universe—part of something bigger—that I might not have ever noticed before. The silence, the solitude, had led the filters to drop off my eyes for a few moments and see the Really Real, to break out of what the spiritual writer Martin Laird refers to as being "trapped behind the wallpaper of my own narrative." That's the same prison that blocks us from seeing clearly the reality around us, that prevents us from experiencing the grace that is operative all around us and within us.

ꟼ

A word about the sources. To avoid repeating these explanations in each meditation, let me give a more ample introduction to some of the personages and texts to which I refer in them. I have already mentioned Bede Griffiths and Abhishiktananda, two Benedictine monks who have been highly influential on my monastic formation. Henri Le Saux (1909–1973) was a French Benedictine monk of St. Anne's in Kergonan in Brittany. His longing for a deeper contemplative life led him to study the mystical literature of India as well as its *sannyasa* tradition, the classic renunciate life, which may be considered an equivalent of Christian monasticism, yet, as he himself would describe it later, more "like Franciscans in the first hour," wanderers and mendicants. He first joined a secular priest and scholar named Jules Monchanin in South India in founding Shantivanam, Saccidananda Ashram (the Ashram of the Holy Trinity) in 1950, with the aim of incorporating the genius of the Indian spiritual tradition with Benedictine monasticism, a true Hindu-Christian experiment. It was there that he assumed the Sanskrit name Abhishiktananda, the "Bliss of the Anointed One." After Monchanin died, and he came more under the spell of the *advaita*/non-dual spirituality of India (which will be explored more later) and Indian sages such as Ramana Maharshi, Poonja, and his own guru, Gnanananda, his interest in Shantivanam waned, and he launched on a very unique path, based more now in North India. He is known for his long anguish in trying to reconcile the truth he felt sure he had experienced of *advaita* with the

"Gregorian peace" of his Christianity. He wrote many books both in French and English and was very influential in the efforts at enculturation in the Indian Catholic Church of the post–Vatican II era as well as in wider Christian circles.

Bede Griffiths (1905–1993) was an Oxford educated Englishman who converted to Christianity, along with his former tutor and close friend C. S. Lewis, in his early twenties. Unlike Lewis though, Bede entered the Roman Catholic communion, and shortly after his baptism also joined Priknash Abbey in the Cotswolds. A voracious reader, he was introduced to Asian thought by an acquaintance who was a first-generation student of Carl Jung. He joined an Indian Benedictine monk in a short-lived experiment in an authentic Indian Benedictine foundation in 1955 near Bangalore, but then with a Belgian Cistercian monk named Francis Acharya founded Kurisumala Ashram in the western state of Kerala, following the ancient Syro-Malabar rite, living a very austere lifestyle. They too adapted their version of *sannyasi*, though in a little more domesticated way than Abhishiktananda, yet still quite strict and ascetic by any standard. When Abhishiktananda wanted to turn Shantivanam over to someone else, Bede became his chosen successor there in 1968. It was there that Bede came into his own and brought Shantivanam to the height of its reputation as the crown jewel of the burgeoning Christian ashram movement in India. His own worldwide reputation grew as well as he wrote several books and was called upon to speak all over the world. He died in 1993, after a series of strokes. It is significant that the World Parliament of Religions, which had not convened since its first iteration in 1893 with Swami Vivekananda's visit to America, was reconvened in 1993 and was dedicated to Fr. Bede as an example of the great marriage of East and West.

Two sacred Indian texts will be mentioned in the following

pages. First, the Upanishads which date back six centuries before the Common Era. The primary and most ancient text for the Hindu tradition are four great tomes called the Vedas. These four works recount mantras and blessings, commentaries on rituals, ceremonies, and sacrifices led by priests of the Brahmin caste. Attached to each of the Vedas are esoteric texts called Upanishads, a word that means "sitting down at the feet of." These do not deal with deities and rituals but concern themselves with the inner journey to the cave of the heart as taught by a guru or teacher. They are more philosophical in nature, dealing with consciousness and ontology (the study of being itself). The major realization for the seers (*rishis*) of the Upanishads is that the ultimate self (*atman*) of the individual is none other than Brahman, the divine ground of being itself. Hence the experience of *advaita*, put simply: God and the human person are "not two," the literal translation of the term.

Another beloved and more popular sacred text in India is the Bhagavad Gita, a name that means literally "the Song of the Lord." It is part of a much larger epic called the Mahabharata, the story of a war of succession between two factions of cousins. The hero of the story is one Prince Arjuna who, before the major battle, discovers that his chariot driver is none other than Lord Krishna, an avatar of the god Vishnu. Krishna then becomes Arjuna's teacher, explaining to him the various yogas—the yoga of action, the yogas of wisdom and renunciation, the yogas of realization and meditation. Some scholars suggest that, though written much earlier, the Gita became more popular among common folk of India around the second century CE because it was more accessible than the sometimes fierce, singular, and impersonal way of the Upanishads, as well as less philosophical and more devotional.

Though both of the aforementioned men knew both of

these texts quite well, I always associate the Upanishads with Abhishiktananda, who was quite convinced of the experience evinced in them. Students of his thought love to point to him saying at one point, "The Upanishads are true. I know it!" One of his most highly regarded books is *The Further Shore*, a treatise on the *sannyasa* tradition, highly respected even by Hindus, that includes an introduction to the Upanishads, the only text that the renunciate ought to read. Bede, in contrast, I easily associate with the Bhagavad Gita, partially because he was bold enough to write a Christian commentary on it, something the great sages of India have done for centuries up 'til the present time. He thought that Abhishiktananda went too far in his emphasis on the *advaita*/non-dual experience and preferred the way of love. Both of these men thought that each of these texts contained great universal wisdom for the spiritual life that could open new horizons for the Christian contemplative as well, new ways to express that core experience of Jesus with his *abba* in which each of us is called to share, outside of using Western terminology.

The other text that you will find mentioned often in the following pages is the classic mystical philosophical Chinese treasure called the Tao te Ching, approximately translated as the "Book of the Power of the Way." Its legendary author is Lao Tzu, a contemporary of the great philosopher Confucius (551–479 BCE), though there is much scholarly doubt about Lao Tzu's actual existence and much speculation that the work is in reality a compilation of aphorisms from an already extant tradition. Be that as it may, the Tao te Ching is the foundational text of an entire cosmology and one of the most commonly translated books in history.

Along with the Tao te Ching in this tradition are the writings of whom we might call Lao Tzu's successor, Chuang Tzu, of whom we have more historical certainty. The major writing attributed to him bears his name, but of the three parts of that work it is only the first part, called "the Inner Chapters," that are considered authentic to him. Whereas Lao Tzu tends to speak from the place of enlightenment post facto, describing the state of attainment, Chuang Tzu carries more of the speculation about and description of the way itself. The work is known for its clever and sometimes humorous wordplay (often lost in translation) and his use of parables, as well as its sharp critique of the prevailing Confucian ethos that was dominant in ancient China.

My major connection to Taoist thought relies on this one fact: I have been convinced by scholars that what the ancient Chinese were trying to convey with the concept of the *tao* is pretty much the equivalent of what the ancient Greeks were trying to convey with the notion of the *logos*, the great divine intelligence behind the cosmos. Of course, it is this Greek notion of the *logos* that Christianity inherits via the Gospel of John who wrote in the Prologue that "In the beginning was the *logos,* and the *logos* was with God, the *logos* was God, and the *logos* was made flesh and dwelt among us," in Jesus.[4] In every Chinese translation of the Bible that I have checked those phrases are rendered, "In the beginning was the *tao*, the the *tao* was with God and the *tao* was God, and the *tao* was made flesh and dwelt among us." And so we can read Taoist literature and learn something in a new way about who we Christians call the Second Person of the Trinity.

As for Buddhist texts, I must admit that I have spent less time with the prime sources (the original Buddhist sutras). My main study has been with the *Dhammapada*, which, being from the third century BCE, is considered one of the earliest as well as most popular Buddhist texts, written in

---

[4] Jn 1:1, 14a.

the ancient language Pali, that attempted to make monastic practice and the Buddha's teachings more accessible; an eighth-century work called *Guide to the Bodhisattva's Way of Life* by Shantideva, especially loved by the Tibetan tradition; and the writings of the founder of Japanese Soto Zen, Dōgen Zenji (1200–1253).

And so you get a glimpse of the enterprise we are undertaking by meditating sacred texts from other traditions, the "work" we do in dialogue. Any citations from these texts will be my own conflations drawn from various translations that I have at my disposal.

❧

One final thought, from the late Scripture scholar, liturgist, and musician Lucien Deiss, whom I was also privileged enough not only to know, but to work for. What he said about music—"The quality of the music you make ought to be as good as the quality of the silence you break"—applies to writing or speaking as well: the most fruitful and truest words come out of the silence and lead us to return there too. When I was studying the techniques of silent meditation, I learned that before anything else one should always remind oneself why we are doing this practice, why we are making the interior journey at all, my intention. I pray that everything I have written here will be part of that "why," and that nothing I have written offends the sacred silence from which it sprang but serves, rather, as inspiration and fodder for your own journey to the cave of the heart.

Holy and Enlightened

On Epiphanies

One day many years ago, one of my brother monks and I were speaking about a third monk—saying nice things, by the way. And I asked the first monk about the other one, "Do you think he's holy?" And he replied, "Yes, but he's not enlightened."

I had never thought of that distinction before, but it made sense as soon as I heard it. I had already been steeping myself in Asian spirituality and mysticism for some time by then, so I understood what he meant. "Enlightened" is a much more common term in Asian mysticism and among New Agers and alternative spiritual seekers, but it's not a part of the typical Christian vocabulary. We usually refer to holiness and holy people.

And yet "enlightenment" is a New Testament word—in Greek *photismos,* sometimes meaning simply "light," but often associated with the light of knowledge. For instance, in the Second Letter to the Corinthians Paul writes about *the light of the gospel of the glory of Christ* and *the light of the knowl-*

edge of the glory of God in the face of Jesus.[1] And in the early church, especially in the writings of Justin Martyr, Irenaeus, and Clement of Alexandria, the word *photismos*/enlightenment was associated directly with baptism. They understood the initiation sacraments themselves as an enlightenment experience that caused a fresh new way of seeing the world and all reality.

The distinction may not apply universally, but I tend to think of holiness as a sweet thing, heart-centered, loving, kind, and charitable, the way of devotion, long-suffering. India would call this the *bhakti marga* and the *karma marga*, the way of devotion and the way of action. Whereas enlightenment is more the *jnana marga*, the way of knowledge. Enlightenment means we have had an experience that makes us see the world in a different way, because we know something new about the world. We have had a glimpse into the true nature of Reality, perhaps like the apostles when they saw Jesus transfigured, and that changes everything. You might think of one of these experiences too as an epiphany, a sudden revelation or insight, when something is revealed or reveals itself. Epiphany is another concept that gets associated with light in the Christian tradition.

Without drawing too fine a line about it, I associate this also with the distinction between knowledge and love, pairing holiness with love and enlightenment with knowledge. Of course, the ideal is that they be brought together, sought together, and experienced together when the intellect allows itself to be flooded with love. That could feasibly be turned around as well: when our love (for God and neighbor) is also filled with wisdom. Wisdom and compassion, *prajña*

---

[1] 2 Cor 4:4, 6.

and *karuna*, always go together in the Buddhist tradition, for instance, like two wings of a bird.

I have heard it said that love goes out, whereas knowledge goes inward. Love is drawn toward beauty, the beauty of another, the beauty of virtue, and the fullness of beauty in God. Love is also drawn toward service. Whereas knowledge is an interior journey toward knowledge of self, our truest self. But I think that is too binary. I think that love is also drawn inward, and wisdom is also drawn outward. And an epiphany, an enlightenment experience, even a revelation of God, usually lets us know more than ourselves in a new way. It's usually wedded to a new insight into others and the world in general.

Consider this extraordinary experience of St. Benedict of Norcia. As St. Gregory the Great recounts it in his *Dialogues,* in the dead of the night, Benedict suddenly beheld "a flood of light shining down from above, more brilliant than the sun, and with it every trace of darkness cleared away." According to Benedict's own description of the vision, "The whole world was gathered up before his eyes in what appeared to be a single ray of light." This is right at the end of Benedict's life. Just before this, he had watched the soul of his beloved twin sister leave her body and enter the court of heaven; and right afterward he saw the soul of his friend Germanus "being carried by angels up to heaven in a ball of fire." It's as if we are seeing Benedict preparing for his own death; perhaps it is a culminating vision of his whole life's journey, a unitive vision. He is seeing with God's eyes, "the whole world . . . in a single ray of light." And yet he has not lost the particular, his sister and his friend.

In his famous autobiography *The Golden String,* Bede Griffiths describes a kind of enlightenment experience when, after a period of fasting and then staying up all night in prayer, for days afterward it was as though he had been given a new power of vision, in which everything seemed to lose its hardness and rigidity and come alive. "The hard casing of exterior reality seemed to have been broken through," he wrote, "and everything disclosed its inner being."

Then there is what is referred to as Thomas Merton's enlightenment experience in Louisville, at the corner of Fourth and Walnut in the center of the shopping district, when he suddenly had the sense that everybody around him was walking around shining like the sun, and he was overwhelmed with the realization that "I loved all those people, that they were mine and I theirs, that we could not be alien to one another even though we were total strangers." He said it was like "waking from a dream of separateness."[2]

What's notable here is how often light is involved in these kinds of experiences. What's also notable is that the world around is not cast off but seen in a new way, along with its inhabitants, in the case of St. Benedict the souls of his sister and friend, for Merton, all the people around him shining like the sun. Merton adds rather ecstatically, "If only we could see each other as we really are all the time." And for Bede, even inanimate things seemed to come alive in a new way.

In the ancient Christian liturgical tradition the Feast of the Epiphany, which is celebrated with all kinds of light— *Jerusalem, your light has come!*—previously celebrated more than Christ being revealed to the nations in the form of the three wise men visiting from the East as it does today. It also celebrated simultaneously Jesus' baptism in the Jordan, which

---

[2] Merton aficionados refer to two other enlightenment experiences in his life, one earlier, a Eucharistic vision during his trip to Cuba, and one later in front of the statues of the sleeping Buddha in Ceylon.

according to the patristic reading sanctified all the waters of the earth, and the wedding feast at Cana, the great icon of the marriage of heaven and earth, the water of our humanity being changed by divine alchemy into the wine of divinity. All three of those are epiphanies.

An enlightenment experience is usually all-encompassing. It changes our understanding of everything, just as Christ's epiphany on earth in all its forms affected everything.

Particularly in Hinduism and Buddhism, there is a marvelous tradition of the "third eye." It is said to be located between the eyebrows (called the *ajna* chakra) and is considered to be the tenth opening of the body. But whereas all the other openings in the body lead out, this one leads in. It is the inner eye of wisdom, the eye that opens when one has achieved enlightenment, *moksha* or *nirvana*. It's sometimes called the *gyananakashu*, "the eye of knowledge," or the seat of the *antarguru,* "the inner teacher." You often see statues of deities or buddhas, famous yogis, sages, and bodhisattvas with some kind of a mark there. Some people who follow Indian traditions wear a mark called a *tilak* at that same spot between the eyebrows to represent this eye of wisdom. At our Christian ashram we too mark ourselves there three times a day, in the morning with sandalwood paste for purity, at noon with red *kumkum* for devotion, and in the evening with white *vibhuti* ash for penance.

Some years ago an acquaintance of mine, who is pretty cynical about Christianity, wrote me at the beginning of Lent saying, "Oh yeah, Ash Wednesday. The day you Christians cover up your third eye with ashes." I thought about it for a minute and then remembered the story in the Gospel of John when Jesus heals a blind man.[3] Jesus does this fantastic

---

[3] Jn 9:12.

visceral gesture: He spits on the ground and makes some mud, and then he smears the spit and mud on the man's eyes and tells him to go wash it off. And when the man did so, he was healed, he could see.

So I wrote back to my sardonic friend, "Yes, we cover up our third eye with ashes for a short time, only to have it washed forty days later in the waters of baptism so that we can really cleanse and open that third eye with the wisdom of resurrection at Easter." I'm not sure it convinced him, but the image stayed with me.

The season of Lent is all about Easter, and Easter is all about baptism. And baptism is all about enlightenment. From ancient times baptisms were normally performed on Easter each year, and there was a preparation period beforehand for the catechumens, those about to be baptized. It was a period of cleansing and formation in which the candidates prepare to die to their old selves and rise to a whole new way of seeing, a new way of living, a new way of being in the world. And the ancient Greek word that was usually associated with both conversion and baptism was again *photismos,* enlightenment or illumination. Baptism was meant to be an enlightenment experience, an epiphany. Baptism is meant to be one of those moments of "sudden Illumination" that encompass and transcend time that T. S. Eliot writes about in "The Four Quartets."

But for most of us Christians, we were baptized when we were infants and have no recollection of the event, let alone any kind of enlightenment experience associated with it. So we too, as Eliot says, "had the experience and missed the meaning." The official teaching of the Church is *ex opere operato,* that the efficacy of the sacrament is operative even just from "the work worked." And yet, even if there was an indelible mark, an ontological change brought about by our having been baptized, it is still not magic. At some point in our spiritual life we need to dedicate our effort to the *ex opere operantis*, to "the working of the work," to uncovering the wisdom that that grace offers us, the new vision it affords us.

I often feel like our spirituality is all about trying to catch up with something that happened to us long ago, to realize a reality that is already somehow operative in the depths of our being. And so not just the period of Lent, but any period of serious spiritual retreat and renewal is a time for the rest of us too, like the fortunate catechumens, to cleanse and purify, die to our old selves (our masks, our false selves, our personas) and realize this enlightened self—cleanse that third eye of wisdom by renewing, remembering, realizing our own death to our old unenlightened self and rising to be a new creation at Easter. *For once you were darkness,* St. Paul says, *but now in the Lord you are light!*[4]

I can point to, and often do, the most significant enlightenment experience in my life. It was the day that I listened to Bede Griffiths give a 45-minute talk in the chapter room of our hermitage in California. I had not yet officially even begun the postulant year of monastic life. It was during what we call a two-month observership. I was mesmerized the entire time he spoke, as much by Bede's presence as by his teaching. But the teaching! All these decades later I am still living off the themes he spoke about that day. I went in one person, and I walked out a different one, with a new way of understanding reality, spirituality, and my humanity. I was almost speechless with the shock of it, as if he had been speaking a language that I didn't even know I knew, teaching about matters in a way that I intuitively knew was right as soon as he said it. It did not make me instantly holy, nor did

---

[4] Eph 5:8.

it make me instantly wise, but it was an epiphany that got me going on a path that I have never left.

Let me give you another example of an enlightenment experience, one I already alluded to, the transfiguration of Jesus and its effects. But I will couch it first in a little framing device.

I got this image from the theologian Ronald Rolheiser. He aptly explained in *The Holy Longing* that a healthy soul has to do two things for us, be both a fire and a container for that fire. First of all, the soul has to "put fire in our veins, keep us energized, vibrant, living with zest." Second, a healthy soul also has to provide a container for that energy, to keep us fixed together. These two functions—the fire and the containment—are like the dance between chaos and order, fire and water, energy and integration, passion and chastity.

A great icon of this for me is the burning bush in Exodus Chapter 3. God is revealed to Moses in the burning bush. The fire, obviously, is the energy, and the bush is a symbol of the container, marvelously unconsumed by the flames, holding the fire without squelching it yet without being destroyed by it.

Another icon of this is Jesus when he was transfigured on Mount Tabor, when his face shone like the sun and even his clothes became white as light. Now Jesus himself has become the burning bush unconsumed by the flames. We get a glimpse of him with what might be called his subtle body, a premonition of his resurrection body, brimming with all the divine energy that it contains, living in the dynamic tension between flesh and divinity.

There's a detail in the Gospel of Luke that always catches my attention. Luke tells us that Peter and his companions who were with Jesus on Mount Tabor were *weighed down with sleep*. The great sages tell us that enlightenment is like waking from sleep, waking from a dream. Could it be that they are having what the Zen tradition calls a sort of *kensho* experience here? Not all the way to the permanent enlightenment, but at least a glimpse of the Really Real. Could it be that Jesus was always like this, and they just could not perceive it? And suddenly they wake up and see what has been there all the time? In his commentary on this feast the third-century writer Origen wrote that matter is by its nature subject to modification and change, and can be turned into anything the Creator wishes, and is capable of taking on any quality that God the great Artificer chooses. So it is no great wonder that at one point we can say that Jesus *had no form or majesty that we should look at him, nothing in his appearance that we should desire him,* as we claim is prophesied about Jesus in the Song of the Suffering Servant in Isaiah.[5] And in the next moment we can say that he was so glorious, majestic, and wondrous that the three disciples "fell on their faces." Jesus' person is both so ordinary and so full of divinity.

But it doesn't end there. My favorite story from the desert monastic tradition is when Abba Lot went to see Abba Joseph and said, "Abba, as far as I can, I say my little office, I fast a little, I pray and meditate, I live in peace and as far as I can, I purify my thoughts. What else can I do?" At that point Abba Joseph stands up, stretches his hands towards heaven, and his fingers became like ten lamps of fire. And Abba Joseph says to Abba Lot, "If you will, you can become all flame!"

We're supposed to access that fire too. We each of us, each one of our souls, is meant to be like that burning bush, our very beings brimming with the energy of the Spirit, unconsumed by the flame. If we want, we could be all flame!

But it doesn't end there either.

---

[5] Is 53:2.

What the Eastern Christian tradition really underlines more than the Western is that while we are working this out for ourselves, we are also working it out for all of creation, preparing a renewal for the entire cosmos. That's the true aim of the spiritual life for a Christian, not contempt for the world, but a re-embrace of it, a transfiguring of the world, enriching creation, as the priests of creation, raising creation to a higher plane, "even to the fullness of a transfigured life," as the Russian philosopher theologian Pavel Florensky says. And not only matter; Saint Basil taught that even time itself is transfigured: The aim of the spiritual life is to live in history and to "transfigure time," to grasp the eternal in the temporal. In other words, everything is meant to be transfigured, nothing gets left behind, *so that God may be all in all.*[6] Ultimately everything is a burning bush. Walter Wink puts it this way: "The gospel is not a message about the salvation of individuals from the world, but of a world transfigured, right down to its basic structures."

I was giving a form of this teaching to some young people in Malaysia, and at the end of the retreat conference I asked, "Does everybody understand what I'm saying?" I have to admit most of the young folks actually looked a little dazed and confused by the whole thing. But my young friend Ian, who was also my host there, suddenly looked me directly in the eyes and said to me, "*Fuiyoh*, Father! Everything's on fire!"[7]

I watched this young man have an enlightenment experience before my very eyes. I was not the cause of it, I was merely an instrument. He was ripe and ready, and I just shared what I had been given, pointed out what was right in front of him. That's right, Ian. Everything's on fire. In Christ, everything's on fire. Poets of course always seem to catch this

---

[6] 1 Cor 15:28.

[7] "Fuiyoh" is an Asian way of expressing amazement, specifically associated with Malaysia.

intuition before the rest of us. Thus Elizabeth Browning's verses: "Earth's crammed with heaven, / And every common bush afire with God; / But only he who sees takes off his shoes, / The rest sit round it and pluck blackberries."

I have been quoting for some years now the old piece of wisdom from Albert Einstein that "no problem can be solved from the same consciousness that created it." The problems that we face as a human race today are not going to be solved by the same consciousness that created those problems in the first place! It is our very choices as human beings that have altered the course of evolution, "God's perfect plan," and so the next step has to be an evolution of our consciousness to a new consciousness, what Bede Griffiths called "a new vision of reality," so that we make better choices. We need a new consciousness, an evolved way of thinking or, as Saint Paul said in the Letter to the Romans, we need to *not be conformed to this world but transformed by the renewal of our minds,*[8] transformed with a new consciousness. So that we can make enlightened decisions.

Where and how do we find this new consciousness, this renewal of our minds? I agree with many who say we can't count on either science and technology nor on institutional religion to do it for us. The transformation cannot come from *outside of us*, it is not going to just be handed to us, especially not top-down. It has to happen *within*. I love how the Franciscan theologian Ilia Delio phrases it. "The head," she says, "has to find a new way to stand in the heart, and the heart must find a new way to stand in God." It's going to be some marvelous combination of knowledge and love, holiness and enlightenment, wisdom and compassion.

It is equally important to add that, as far as I am concerned, the only real engine of that transformation, that evolution

---

[8] Rom 12:2.

of our consciousness, the only real agent of the renewal of our minds, is from what I call deep practice. Of course, in my religious bias I say that it is through the Spirit and the spiritual life, specifically suggesting that this transformation can only happen through meditation, prayer, and a renewal of the contemplative dimension of our spirituality—as individuals, communally, as a church.

And by the way, no politician or world leader, on the right or the left, has the solution to the problems we face unless they are doing this deep work too.

We Western Christians are remarkably good at action—the works of holiness. I swell with pride at the fact that whenever there are disasters in the world—famines, floods, refugee crises, wars—Christians, and especially, I must say, Catholic women religious, are in the front line. I would never downplay the corporal works of mercy. As we hear several times in the Letter of James, *faith without works is dead.*[9] Full stop.

But our works, including our corporal works of mercy, are often, in medical terms, more like triage and palliative care, not solutions to the problems themselves. And ministers and missionaries must often feel as if they are like MASH units[10] behind the front lines yelling up to the infantry, "Can you stop sending us so many dead and wounded?! Can you stop sending us so many poor and homeless? So many starving and naked? So many environmental and economic refugees? Can you stop sending us so many victims of racism and bigotry? So many young people already emotionally scarred and dysfunctional?"

But these problems are not going to be, cannot be, solved with the same consciousness that created the problems. Just

---

[9] Jas 2:14–26.
[10] Acronym for "Mobile Army Surgical Hospital."

as the Letter of James says that faith without works is dead, so works without faith are also going to die, and I mean the deep abiding faith, the transformation of our minds and our very beings that can only come about through prayer and meditation, through the spiritual life. Just observe the burnout rate among youth ministers and other ministries in the church, let alone the crisis in the clergy. I'm sure other spiritual traditions experience their own version of this. Without deep spirituality, without the fresh new spiritual way of thinking that comes about through the way of interiority, eventually we become like cars running with no oil in the engine: We seize up, burn out, we grow bitter, we wind up pushing our own agendas rather than the gospel, or we become merely licensed professionals—academics, musicians, authors, social workers, experts in our fields—rather than spiritual servant-leaders.

I have always thought that in the Catholic Church we make too sharp a dividing line between the active and the contemplative life. Mind you, there will always be personalities suited to one or the other, as there will always be places of pure contemplation for the sake of and salvation of the world, for the rest of the Body that is too busy to stop. But that sharp division, as Jesus says about Moses's allowance for a man to give a certificate of dismissal to his wife, that sharp division between the active and the contemplative life was only given to us because of the hardness of our hearts.[11]

The world needs us to be holy, but it also needs us to be enlightened. The seminal twentieth-century German theologian Karl Rahner famously wrote that "the Christian of the future will be a 'mystic,' one who has experienced 'something,' or will cease to be anything at all." By "mystic" I'm certain he meant a person who had had a genuine experience of the

---

[11] Mt 19:8; Mk 10:4.

Divine emerging from the very heart of their existence. And with this Rahner is moving mysticism from the margins of Christian life to its very center. What we have witnessed in the hunger of so many of our brothers and sisters who have left Christianity and gone to traditions that favor the contemplative life and the way of interiority is that mysticism is not reserved for a few privileged people, but ought to be a feature of people's everyday experience as they live out the enlightenment experience that was, is, could be our baptism, our immersion into the Paschal mystery of dying and rising with Christ. The ancients certainly thought so.

There's an interesting play on words in St. Paul's Letter to the Colossians in the Greek. Paul writes, *When Christ who is your life is revealed, then you will also be revealed with him in glory.*[12] More literally it is "When the *christos phanerōthē* arrives—that's the same root as for the word *epiphany*—then your *phanerōthēsthe* will happen." If it weren't so awkward we could translate that as "when Christ epiphanies, you will epiphany too." Saint John says it in his own way: *Beloved, we are God's children now; what we will be has not yet been revealed. What we do know is this: when he is revealed, we will be like him, for we will see him as he is.*[13] When Christ's epiphany happens, our epiphany will happen too. When the full understanding of who Jesus Christ was and is happens in us, when we understand what it means to have been baptized into the Paschal Mystery of death and rebirth, then we will also realize who we are and what the world around us is—"charged," in the words of Gerard Manley Hopkins, "with the grandeur of God."

One final thought: I never can seem to memorize them,

---

[12] Col 3:6.
[13] 1 Jn 3:2.

and I need to look them up every single time, but that notwithstanding I love Saint Paul's teaching on the fruits of the Spirit in the Letter to the Galatians and I feel like I could work them into any and every teaching or sermon. It's simply this: *The fruit of the Spirit is love, joy, peace, patience, kindness, generosity, faithfulness, gentleness, and self-control.*[14] This to me is the ultimate litmus test for everything.

For everything!

If a Christian is trying to convince me of his or her interpretation or practical application of something, and I don't see these things being manifested, I just nod politely and walk away. And the same applies to any teacher from any other tradition, be that a yoga instructor, an imam, or a monastic of any tradition. However, if I see these virtues being manifested in anyone of any faith tradition or none at all, I want to bow down and kiss their feet because I know that the Spirit of God is present, maybe in some new and unexpected way.

Let me end with the opposite of what I started with: I've met people whom I thought were enlightened but who were so cold or haughty, sometimes even pretentious and rude, seemingly detached from their own or anyone else's humanity. What I am looking for in others and in my own life is the marriage of wisdom and compassion, and for whatever enlightenment I may be graced with to always manifest as loving, joyful, peaceful, patient, kind, generous, faithful, and gentle, and to give me the virtue of self-control.

Then I will know that it is truly of the Spirit.

---

[14] Gal 5:22–23.

2

This Is My Beloved

On Baptism

There's a famous story from India about a lioness who was about to give birth. She was going around in search of prey heavy with child when she saw a flock of sheep and pounced on them. Unfortunately for her, she was shot with an arrow by the shepherd in the effort. And she gave birth to a little baby lion in the midst of the sheepfold and then died right there. So the baby lion was born motherless, but it wound up being taken care of by the sheep, and they brought it up like a sheep. It grew up with the sheep; it ate grass, and it bleated like a sheep. And even though in time it became a full-grown lion, it always thought it was a sheep.

One day another lion came along in search of prey and was astonished to see this young lion in the midst of a sheepfold and running away scared like the other sheep at the approach of danger. The other lion kept trying to get near the sheep-lion to tell it that it wasn't a sheep after all but really a lion, but the poor animal ran away every time the other lion came near. One day the other lion found the sheep-lion asleep in the grass, and snuck up on it, terrifying it and holding it down with its mighty paws. And it kept saying, "You are a lion. Why are you running around like a sheep?" But the other lion (who thought it was a sheep) just cried all the more, "I am a sheep! Leave me alone! Leave me alone!" And it bleated and bleated because it couldn't believe anything to the contrary. So, the other lion (who knew it was a lion) grabbed the first lion (who didn't know it was a lion) by the scruff of the neck and dragged it to a pool of water, and said, "Look here: there's my reflection and there's yours. You're a lion!" The young sheep-lion looked at its own reflection and then looked at the other lion and then looked at its own reflection again. And in a flash came the shocking revelation that it too was actually a lion.

And it roared—the bleating was gone for good.

∽

All four Gospels tell the story of Jesus' baptism in the Jordan. Here is Mark's pithy version of it.

> In those days Jesus came from Nazareth of Galilee and was baptized by John in the Jordan. And just as he was coming up out of the water, he saw the heavens torn apart and the Spirit descending like a dove on him. And a voice came from heaven, "You are my Son, the Beloved; with you I am well pleased."[1]

One of the things I find notable about this story of Jesus' baptism is what comes right after it. For me the timeline is very important. Right after Jesus' baptism in the Jordan, he is going to be led by the Holy Spirit into the desert. And then he will begin his public ministry of preaching and healing. All

---

[1] Mk 1:9–11.

three of the synoptic Gospels record it in that order: baptism, desert, ministry.[2]

I tend to think of the desert experience that follows Jesus' baptism, those forty days of fasting and prayer, as his rite of passage, like an archetypal initiation ritual, if you will. But he can't do that—or at least he *doesn't* do that, he doesn't face the desert—until he has experienced what he experiences in the Jordan.

And what does he experience in the Jordan? This one very important thing: He hears his Father say, "You are my beloved one, with whom I am well pleased."

But let's start at the beginning. Remember God's self-revelation in the desert to Moses in the burning bush as recorded in the Book of Exodus? That's when we learn God's name, the great *tetragrammaton*: *I AM WHO AM*. Thomas Aquinas and many Christian thinkers who follow him will interpret this to mean *Deus es esse*—God is Being itself. (Note: not *a* being, not even the greatest being in a hierarchy of beings, but Being itself—*esse ipsum*.) We believe that God and Being are the same thing: God is Being; God is I AM! (The Spanish theologian Raimundo Panikkar, who loved to play with language, wrote that we shouldn't even say "God is" but "God *Am*.")

Well, at the Jordan, God (imaged as Father here) gives that same I AM to Jesus. God says to Jesus, "*You* are! You are Beloved! You are my delight! You are powerful! You are precious! You are free! You are so beautiful! You *are!* So—breathe! Thunder! Be!" God loves Jesus into being, and Jesus has such an awareness of himself as beloved that he can take that I AM as his own. In John 10 Jesus declares that *'The Father is in me, and I am in the Father.'* He is able to say in another

---

[2] Mt 3:13–17; Lk 3:21–22. Jn 1:29–34 does not mention the desert experience.

place, *'I am the way. I am the truth. I am the life.'*[3] And six other times in that same gospel, once while he is being led away to his death, he simply says, *'I AM.'* In John 8, for example, when Jesus is debating with his co-religionists, he says it twice, seeming to equate himself with the I AM of God, culminating in him saying a third time *'Before Abraham was I AM.'*[4] If there were any doubt as to how his fellow Jews might have understood that, they picked up stones to throw at him because that sounded like blasphemy to them. But it wasn't blasphemy; it was the truth. God was in Jesus and Jesus was in God. God gave Jesus not only his own existence; God gave Jesus the I AM! Being itself.

Then, and only then, does Jesus go—or is Jesus led—into the desert. It is because Jesus knew his own dignity as a son of God that he was filled with the strength of the Spirit and could face that desert and then go on to give his life over to his ministry of healing and preaching. It is because Jesus knew he was a child of God that he could heal the sick, walk on water, raise the dead. It is because Jesus knew his own dignity as an offspring of God that he could walk amid the poorest of the poor, the lepers, the homeless, the prostitutes and drunks, and not feel the slightest bit squeamish or worried about his ritual purity. Jesus has all that power because he knows his oneness with God.

And in his final discourse in the Gospel of John he extends that oneness by telling his friends, *'I am in the Father and you in me and I in you.'*[5] Christ is also in us, particularly, if not for any other reason, by the Spirit of the Risen Christ that we receive at our baptism. Abhishiktananda's insight into this was that just as Jesus identified with the I AM of God, by

---

[3] Jn 14:6.
[4] Jn 8:21–30; 58. Again repeated in the final discourse of John, 13:19.
[5] Jn 10:31–42; 14:11, 20.

virtue of our baptism so we come to—ought to, are called to—identify with the I AM of Jesus. The Father gives it to Jesus; Jesus gives it to us.

And like Jesus, neither can we face the deserts in our lives until we have that. This is what our baptism, our initiation into the love life of the Trinity, was supposed to have been for us.

Unfortunately, instead we often get the whole thing, and religion itself, all backwards. We keep thinking that if we just obey the rules, follow the laws, if we just behave right, God will love us. We keep using religion that way too, as a kind of moral superstructure. Then we spend a lot of time wagging our finger at each other, scolding and disapproving. Well, if it were true that it's in our power to earn our salvation and make God love us, what's the point in that? If that were true, what would we need God for? Love, like grace itself, is not something you can earn. That may be something we have learned from our parents, or from our schools, or from social media, but the truth is we cannot earn God's love by doing something.

Right behavior doesn't come first. Love comes first. It is God's love that is the power behind right behavior, just as grace, the love of God poured into our hearts, gives us the ability to live uprightly. St. Paul was clear about this. He came to understand that even the Law of Moses, which Paul, a good observant Jew, turned his back on, has no power! Rules have no power. Moral exhortations have no power. The Catechism of the Catholic Church has no power. And neither does knowledge, by the way, as any addict would tell you. Otherwise, why would so many people keep doing things that lead to their death, like smoking, overeating, and drugging themselves to death?

Only love has power. And knowing that we are beloved, precious, beautiful—that's real power.

Jesus passes that I AM, that "You are my beloved," on to us. The fourth-century bishop and Doctor of the Church Hilary of Poitiers taught that the voice of God "made itself heard over Christ at the moment of his baptism, so as to reach humanity on earth by means of him and in him: 'This is my Beloved!'" Jesus did not receive this title for himself, Cyril says; he received that title "to give its glory to us." At our baptism we are told "You are! You are Beloved! You are so beautiful! You are my delight! You are powerful! You are precious and free! You are!" Just as Jesus knew his Father's love and knew his own dignity and so could face the desert, we too can be filled with that Holy Spirit and face the deserts of our lives, because that is our dignity as well, branches grafted onto the vine. Just as Jesus' power to heal the sick, walk on water, and raise the dead flowed from the realization of his own goodness, so we can do even greater things, Jesus says, because that is our dignity as well. If it is because Jesus knew his own dignity that he could walk amid the poorest of the poor, so we too can lay our lives down for the world if we are secure in our own dignity as well, knowing that every hair on our head is numbered and counted.

The problem is, of course, that we don't know that. We don't remember or we never heard that message that was meant for us. Those words that were called out over us too do not echo in our ears, or else they are drowned out by the noise of the dysfunction, clamor, and confusion that surrounds us. And so many of us spend our lives walking around looking in store windows and reading self-help books and staring into other people's eyes asking over and over again in a thousand different ways, "Am I? Am I smart enough? Am I pretty enough? Am I young enough? Talented enough?"

Why? Why do we not have a sense of our own dignity? Worse than that, why can't we give that sense of dignity to each other? Why is that often parents can't pass it on to their children? Do they not have it themselves? Why are we so afraid to tell each other how beautiful we are? Is it because we do not know it about ourselves? Does it hurt me so much to tell you? Can I not see it in you, because I can't see it in myself?

The good news is, we get a chance each year to renew that voice over our own heads. Because, though the celebration of Easter is at first glance simply about Jesus rising from the dead, *liturgically* it's all about baptism, baptism of new catechumens and the renewal of our own baptismal vows. And we could think of the baptismal font as if it were a reflecting pool like the one in the story about the lion who thought it was a sheep. At least that's the way article #537 of the Catechism of the Catholic Church explains it. "Everything that happened to Christ lets us know that, after the bath of water, the Holy Spirit swoops down upon *us* from high heaven and that, adopted by the Father's voice, we become children of God."

Jesus, the Lion of Judah, through the Church, drags us to the banks of that reflecting pool and says, "Look: there is my reflection and there is yours. This is who you are: the image of God, a capacity for the Infinite. This is who you are: a temple of the Holy Spirit, a well-spring of life-giving water, and you can have the same relationship with the Father that I have. This is who you are: the Beloved One. This is who you are: God's daughter, God's son, the one in whom God delights. This is who you are: an heir of the kingdom, the glory of God. This is who you are!"[6]

There's another famous saying in this regard, from Saint Clare of Assisi. As she put it, Jesus "is the brightness of eternal light and the mirror without a cloud." And so, she writes, "Look into that mirror every day and study well your reflec-

---

[6] Most of these "affirmations" are taken from the "Litany of the Person" written by an anonymous source.

tion." Look at who you are! Look into the baptismal reflecting pool every day and study well your reflection.

Furthermore, this is what we can do and be for each other. This is what being church could be and should be—the place where we hear over and over again the story of our dignity as children of God, as Beloved, and then be able to look into each other's eyes with the eyes of Christ, and reflect back to each other not our projections, not our needs, not what we wish the world and each other to be, but to reflect back "You are the Beloved." And that would be power for us to build a world of justice and peace, one heart at a time. It seems to me Christianity at its best can and should be this kind of mirror, even this kind of mother (we do speak about "Holy Mother the Church"), just as the baptismal pool becomes a reflecting pool of Jesus' own glory. No matter what kind of upbringing one has had, good or bad nurturing, there should always be the community of believers in Jesus that see each other and reflect to one another each other's being in the image of God, beloved, beautiful, precious and free.

That's the good news. But there's a hard lesson in here too. Just as when we celebrate Good Friday we don't ever forget Easter Sunday and the joy of the victory that is already won, so also when we celebrate Easter, we ought to never forget Good Friday. There's a way of the cross that has led to this and leads to this. Something has got to die before we discover our real selves *hidden with Christ in God.*[7]

What has to die? That part of us that thinks it's a lamb instead of a lion. No, better: that part of us that *prefers* to be a lamb, that prefers to remain in our comfortable illusions. The sheep in the fable is a symbol of the stories we tell ourselves about ourselves, the narrative we cling to. What has to die is our lethargy, our laziness, our apathy, our cowardice, our false

---

[7] Col 3:14.

selves. (In Sarah Ruden's translation of the Gospels, which I love, she renders Jesus saying in John 14:27, "Do not let your hearts be troubled, and do not let them be cowardly.")

What has to die is our bleating like helpless little lambs.

The hard part of the good news is that the entrance ticket to our real self is baptism—or at least some kind of baptism. And baptism is a symbol of death before it is a symbol of new life, a symbol of drowning. As Paul says in the Letter to the Romans:

> Do you not know that all of us who have been baptized into Christ Jesus were baptized into his death? Therefore we have been buried with him by baptism into death, so that, just as Christ was raised from the dead by the glory of the Father, so we too might walk in newness of life.[8]

It's almost as if Jesus had not only to immerse himself in water first (at his own baptism) but even allow himself to drown in it—drown in the sea of human pain to show us that dying will not kill us. Of course, we believe that Jesus didn't *have to* die to anything since his will was perfectly only to do God's will. But for *us* to live out our baptismal newness of life, for us to access this precious divinity within us, we have to die constantly, a little every day. Because it's only by drowning gracefully that we can walk the roads of earth with ease and grace as disciples of Jesus. It is only by something in us dying that we can access all that is promised to us by the best of our spiritual tradition—being divinized, participating in the divine nature, owning our real inheritance, becoming who we are.

When I was in high school, we used to gather at a friend of mine's house on the weekends before we'd head out for

---

[8] Rom 6:3–11.

some evening of teenage revelry. And I will never forget what my friend's father would say to his son—and to all of us by extension—as we headed out the door: "Remember who you are!" Those were and are powerful words. Living up to that is a whole lot more attractive than shrinking under the withering stare of a moralizing scold. Especially if we know that who we are is so filled with dignity.

I never tire of the meditation from Marianne Williamson that Nelson Mandela quoted when he was inaugurated as president of South Africa.

> Our deepest fear is not that we are inadequate. Our deepest fear is that we are powerful beyond measure. It is our light, not our darkness, that most frightens us. We ask ourselves: "Who am I to be brilliant, talented, fabulous?" Actually, who are you *not* to be? You are a child of God!

This is the line I love, and I usually almost shout it when I quote it: "Your playing small does not serve the world!"

Maybe in keeping with the fable above we could say that our deepest fear is not that we are sheep. Our deepest fear is that we are lions, powerful beyond measure. It's not our own power, mind you: It's the power of the Spirit that has been poured into the fragile earthen vessel of our being, but poured into us it is. We are powerful because we are powered by the Spirit of God with, as the prophet Isaiah tells us, the Spirit's gifts of wisdom, understanding, counsel, knowledge—and fortitude.[9]

Our playing small does not serve the world!

---

[9] Is 11:1–2.

Postscript

I was ordained through and for our monastic community after I made solemn vows as a monk, and my priestly formation did not include a lot of the pastoral training that most priests get. So I had very little pastoral experience outside of celebrating the sacraments within our small monastic community and for our guests. About six years after I was ordained, I was living away from my community for an extended period of time in a small urban area on the central coast of California, a very progressive college town. I wasn't there often because my own work was largely an itinerant ministry. But during that period, I volunteered to fill in as the parish priest for a friend of mine named Mark with whom I had attended seminary while Mark took a much-needed seven-month sabbatical. It was a marvelous experience for me, immersed for the first time in the daily life of a wonderful, engaged community, really nothing short of a love affair, we all got along so well. Of course, I was excused from all the administrative duties that most parish priests have to attend to, which made it even sweeter. All I had to do was preside and preach, and some limited pastoral ministry.

It happened that the last Sunday of that period was the Solemnity of the Baptism of the Lord. I really wanted to convey one last strong message to the good people of that parish, because I felt as if we had really made a journey together the prior six months. I shared with them a much shorter version of what I have written above, but I then went somewhat longer than I usually do and added some stuff that was more uncharacteristically self-referential than I usually do in a homily.

I recounted to them that the first time I had presided at

Mass there before that sabbatical period had actually been on Ash Wednesday the previous year. And it just so happened that a reporter and photographer from the local newspaper showed up that day, wanting to do a story about the beginning of Lent. And they wanted to take my picture distributing ashes to accompany the article. Now, I had been living in that city for over a year at that point, but I was anonymous: Very few knew I was a monk or a priest. I was a little reluctant to surrender my anonymity. However, even more pressing than that, I knew that the next day a major report was going to be released detailing the extent of the sex abuse crisis among the clergy in California. I myself had been greatly shaken by that crisis, and I certainly did not want my photo in priestly garb splashed on the pages of the paper next to an article detailing the sex abuse crisis in the Church. (We compromised by agreeing that the caption would read, "a visiting monk" instead of "the substitute priest.")

I still have the notes from that homily. I ended it with these words.

> People in ministry have their own moments struggling with the efficacy of the institution and hierarchy and bureaucracy of the Church, and many times wonder if it wouldn't be better to get out of the system and go be a social worker instead. Why do they stay? When I was in the monastery, I often wondered why so many of my diocesan priest friends like Fr. Mark stayed—it seems so difficult for them and so lonely. Now after two years wandering around the world preaching and singing, and six months serving here as your priest I know, I know why we stay.
>
> For you. We stay for you! Because you are so beautiful, and we want to make sure someone is here to tell you.

3

Bread for the Journey

On Becoming Eucharist

The human psyche has a hard time holding tension, allowing for multidimensionality and multivalence. We prefer responses that are neat and to the point; we like our solutions black and white. But that makes it hard to truly appreciate the depth dimensions that there are to the Sacrament of the Eucharist in the liturgical traditions of Christianity. The Eucharist holds a broad range of meanings that at times seem to be in tension with each other. Of course, another way of saying that and thinking about it, and this to my mind is preferable, is that these various levels of meaning, these tensions, are not contradictory but complementary, and they give us a fuller picture of this most fundamental and archetypal of Christian sacraments.

One basic tension in the Liturgy of the Eucharist is between sacrifice and meal. Which one is it? Or, better, since it is obviously both—a sacrificial meal—which aspect should we accentuate? Having been raised in what I like to think of as the best of the intelligent moderate progressive tradition of Catholicism after Vatican II, my tendency would be to lean on the side of the meal. That's the aspect that got brought into much higher relief in the *Novus Ordo*, the reformed liturgy of Vatican II. That's when the altars got turned around, and the priest began once again facing the assembly as in the most ancient times instead of facing in the same direction as the people, normally toward the East (*ad oriens*), with his back to them. At that point the high altars often also gave way to something more resembling a table, even if a large one. This is not even to mention all the other moves toward the vernacular, and I mean by the "vernacular" much more than simply language: music, vesture, and simplified and enculturated ceremony.

Having grown up with Mass around the coffee table in our living room with groups of my parents' friends, and having celebrated Eucharist in many other intimate informal but nonetheless sacred settings—on beaches, at retreat centers, in a hotel room in Israel using a guitar case for an altar, alone on the floor of my room at an ashram in Rajpur in north India, with no Catholic church (or Catholic) in sight, using a chapati and some very strange tasting wine—I am very attuned to how sacred the simple and intimate can be, sometimes more sacred, at least to my taste, than ornate high church ceremonies that often have felt disembodied, haughty, artificial, and impersonal.

In this regard I have often thought of Teilhard de Chardin's consecratory prayer from his "Mass on the World" which was written first on the battlefield of Verdun where he was serving as a stretcher bearer, and completed later on the steppes of Mongolia when he had no bread, no wine, no missal:

I, your priest, will make the whole earth my
   altar—
And on it I will offer you all the labors and suffer-
   ings of the world . . .

I will place on the paten the harvest to be won by
    labor . . .
Into my chalice I will pour all the sap which is to
    be pressed out this day from the Earth's fruits.

As the French liturgist Louis-Marie Chauvet explains, when
we take up elements from our daily lived experience—food
and drink, water and oil, even words and gestures—and use
them in a liturgical ritual setting, using ordinary things in an
extraordinary way, what we are really doing is negotiating the
relationship between the human and the divine. Performing
a ritual with ordinary items causes a kind of jarring rupture
with the ordinary. And it is just that rupture that can put
us at the threshold of the sacred. Think of the yearly Seder
meal or even the meal on every shabbat up to this very day
in Jewish households and as far back as Jesus' last meal with
his disciples when he did something new with, and said
something startling (and memorable) about, the bread and
the wine at the end of the meal. Just so in the sacrificial
meal that is the Eucharist: placing ordinary items in a ritual
context can lead us to liminal experiences, "on a sometimes
barely perceptible sensory threshold." It's a delicate balance
and a fine art, finding just the right proportion of ordinary
and ritual. If there is not enough break from the ordinary
or if there is too little relation to the ordinary, either way we
lose the power of the ritual.

One other tension in the Eucharist lies between an accent
on the Real Presence or, if I may use the word, the "static"
presence of Christ in the consecrated host, as contrasted with
an accent on the *action* of Eucharist. By "action" I mean both
our full active conscious participation in the eucharistic liturgy (not simply as passive attendees) as well as our *becoming*
Eucharist. As Pope St. Leo the Great prayed (in case you're

already wondering about my orthodoxy), "Change us into what we receive." Saint Augustine too heard God tell him that unlike most food which is changed into ourselves, God says that in consuming the Eucharist, "I will change you into me." Again, my prejudice is toward the latter, full, conscious, and active participation rather than an exclusive accent on the Real Presence. At the same time, in the years living with my monastic community on the central coast of California I rarely missed the evening time with my brothers and our guests meditating, adoring in the presence of the Blessed Sacrament ensconced in a humble monstrance. And whenever I travel to a foreign city and walk its streets, as is my wont, I always look for a Catholic church and find the Eucharistic chapel, and even search out places that have Exposition and/ or Perpetual Adoration so I can bask in the Presence of this great sign of Christ Jesus' enduring presence.

It may come as no surprise that I am going to make an argument here for active and conscious participation, not only in the liturgy itself but upon walking out the doors of the church, and how that is an essential part of our participation—to *be* Eucharist. But I may surprise you by first making an argument for a re-emphasis on the sacrificial aspect of the Eucharistic meal.

There's a reason that our liturgical tradition keeps the notion of eucharist-as-meal in tension with eucharist-as-sacrifice. On the one hand, there certainly can be a downside to an overemphasis on the sacrificial element that may have something to do with the era in which the accent on sacrifice came to higher prominence. James Carroll, writing about the rise of the imperial church under Constantine in the fourth century in his captivating book *Jerusalem, Jerusalem,* explained how in that era Christian cultic practice in general began to shift decisively. The Eucharist began to be celebrated on altars in large basilicas that replicated and adopted the aesthetics of the pagan temples of antiquity. This is when the Eucharist, which had originally been a joyful meal shared over tables in home churches, started to be referred to more as the "sacrifice of the Mass." The greater emphasis on sacrifice in turn also highlighted the institution of priesthood more, which neatly served the aspirations of a newly empowered hierarchy under a now-sympathetic emperor and empire. Carroll is especially critical of this whole historical trend, claiming that this more sacrificial Mass then subtly encouraged priests to see themselves above the laity and consequently "infected the Eucharistic theology with magic, resuscitating many of the characteristic abuses of a material sacrificial cult."

That is a bit of an extreme spin on it, but not an uncommon view. And there is a profound verifiable truth in that argument going back to the earliest literature of the church. The first-century Syrian liturgical document known as the *Didache*, for instance, which is a foundational document in the history of the liturgy, places the emphasis on life much more than on death in its eucharistic prayer, and it doesn't refer to the crucifixion at all.

At the same time, the overemphasis on "meal" also has its downsides. As the late liturgist Aidan Kavanagh pointed out years ago, to know Christ sacramentally only in terms of bread and wine is to know Christ only partially, "in the dining room as host and guest." It's a valid enough knowledge, but it may be too civil. "However elegant the knowledge of the dining room may be, it begins in the soil, in the barnyard, in the slaughterhouse." However warm it is to gather round the dinner table, every meal begins "amid the quiet violence of the garden, strangled cries, and fat spitting in the pan. Table manners depend on something's having been grabbed by the throat." In other words, we can easily forget that *every meal* is a sacrifice. We are pretty far removed from the reality of our food, from the sources of our nourishment. It comes to us in plastic containers, out of drive-through windows, processed and neat and refined. We generally have no sense at all that every meal involves a sacrifice.

There's another passage from the liturgist and author Nathan Mitchell that I never tire of quoting. He says that part of the disadvantage of exaggerating the notion of Eucharist as "banquet," for instance, is that "banquets suggest abundance, lavish excess of food and drink—almost as though the eucharist were a luxury meal for wealthy gourmands. This image is strongly appealing of course in an affluent American culture of conspicuous consumption." The image of a banquet is very attractive to a culture that has pie-eating and hot-dog-eating contests and where there are so-called "gut-busting restaurants" where you can get your meal for free if you can eat some ghastly amount of food. I found one such meal that starts with a 36-ounce certified Angus bone-in Tomahawk ribeye steak, but you also need to eat a baked potato, French fries, side salad, and dinner roll with butter in 15 minutes, "no sharing and no bathroom breaks!" Also, the steak must be eaten "clean to the bone." Some may find this kind of humorous; I find it repulsive, nearly obscene when you think, as Mitchell points out, that there are millions of people on our planet "who would give their last scrap of clothing for a single cup of rice." According to the United Nations, an estimated 9 million people die of hunger each year, between 19,000 and 24,000 a day, 10,000 of them children. Meanwhile, as I write this, according to the American Centers for Disease Control, the US obesity prevalence has increased from 30.5% to 42.4%, and morbid obesity has increased from 4.7% to 9.2%. I loved *Babette's Feast* as much as anyone but there's got to be more to it than that. (And think of what Babette sacrificed to put on that banquet—everything!)

Two images from the Jewish Scriptures that get associated with the Eucharist come to mind. The first is from the Book of Exodus, when the wandering Jews were falling into despair for lack of food and God sent them manna.[1] In what is known as the Bread of Life Discourse in chapter 6 of the Gospel of John, Jesus alludes to this manna several times. There's an important aspect to this manna that we would do well to remember. God commanded that they should gather it, as much as each could eat. And so they did; some of them gathered a lot of it and some only gathered a little. But when they measured what they had gathered, those who had gathered a lot had nothing left over, while those who had gathered only a little had no lack. Moses had also told them that they were supposed to gather only as much as they thought they could eat in one sitting and not save any of it till the morning. But, of course, some of the people didn't obey and kept some overnight. And the manna that was left till the morning was found to be rotten and full of worms. Every morning they again gathered as much as they could eat at one sitting. But if anyone was tempted to hold on to it and stuff it in their backpacks for later, they were out of luck, because when the sun grew hot, it melted.

In other words, there was just enough for the day.

Another reading from the Jewish Scriptures related to the Eucharist is in 1 Kings,[2] where we see someone falling into the same kind of despair. Queen Jezebel is hunting Elijah down to kill him, and Elijah is praying for death. He falls asleep under a broom tree and enters into a dream realm where he

---

[1] Ex 16:16–21.
[2] 1 Kgs 19:1–9.

is twice greeted by an angel who brings him nourishment. Elijah is heading to Horeb, the mountain where he will have his epiphany in the sound of sheer silence, and this food will be his strength for the forty days and forty nights that it will take him to cross the desert to get there. It is surely from this reading that we get the tradition of calling the Eucharist "bread for the journey."

You can't help but see an allusion to the forty years of the Israelites in the desert and Jesus' own forty days fasting and praying. But like the Israelites in the desert, so too here with Elijah, the key is in the emptiness. When the Israelites were really hungry and ready to rely solely on God, God feeds them, with just enough for the day, nothing extra. And when Elijah has been emptied of his own strength and reached the limits of his own power, the crisis of his limitations, God feeds him.

Perhaps we only truly appreciate the power of the Eucharist when we are that hungry, when we are that poor. *'Blessed are the poor in spirit.'* In the days to come it might just be the poor themselves who will lead the way, and with them will be those who know how to live close to the earth, and those who know how to live simply. It may be they who will be teaching the rest of us how to survive. All these things that we have stored up for ourselves, all the things that we have come to consider as our rights and our standard of living are suddenly going to seem like what they are to much of the rest of the world—luxury items that we have been gorging ourselves on. And that may apply to our access to the Eucharist too, as we all learned during the lockdowns of the Covid period. We have been spoiled in the so-called developed world up 'til now. By necessity we may have to learn to live simpler and more gently on the earth, and learn to content ourselves with just enough for the day. (I often think that this too is why we are so in need of the wisdom of our

First Nation peoples, who know better how to live close to the land.) And then, when we are down to the basics, when we are empty and close enough to death, we will really learn what the Eucharist is—bread for the journey.

We are supposed to *come* hungry, but we're also supposed to *leave* a little lean as well, with just enough food for the journey, just enough strength for the day, as the Israelites learned about the manna. As Jesus tells the disciples to take nothing extra with them on the road to spreading his word. Our daily bread—the bread we need, no more, no less.

Many years before he became the Bishop of Rome, a young theologian named Joseph Ratzinger wrote that "Communion is not a prize for those who are particularly virtuous—who, in that case, could receive it without being a Pharisee?" (I quoted that often when the great debates were circulating in our country about whether we could deny Communion to certain people.) No, instead, Ratzinger says, Communion is "the bread of pilgrims that God offers to us in this world, offers us in our weakness."

❧

And now, what do we mean by "becoming Eucharist"?

There's an instructive story in the Gospel of Luke.[3] The day was drawing to a close, and the apostles came to Jesus and told him to send the crowd away so that the people could go into the surrounding villages and countryside to lodge and get provisions, because they were in a deserted place.

But he said to them, "You give them something to eat."
They said, "We have no more than five loaves and two

---

[3] Lk 9:12–17. It has a parallel in the Gospel of Matthew 14 and Mark 6.

fish—unless we are to go and buy food for all these people." For there were about five thousand men. And he said to his disciples, "Make them sit down in groups of about fifty each." They did so and made them all sit down. And taking the five loaves and the two fish, he looked up to heaven, and blessed and broke them, and gave them to the disciples to set before the crowd. And all ate and were filled. What was left over was gathered up, twelve baskets of broken pieces.

There are so many interesting features in this story that allude to the Eucharistic mystery: the notion of multiplication and abundance, for instance; the use of fish—it's amazing that for all the times that fish gets mentioned in connection to Eucharist that we didn't wind up with Holy Communion being bread and fish instead of bread and wine! I also love the image of "twelve baskets of broken pieces." It's hard to miss the allusion to the twelve tribes and the twelve apostles. But I especially find "twelve baskets of broken pieces" to be a marvelous image for the church.

One other little detail though is especially in high relief in the Gospel of Matthew, where this same story is told twice, once with Jesus feeding five thousand and again when he feeds four thousand, but Jesus only says this in the first version as he does here in Luke's version: When the twelve came to Jesus and told him to send the crowd away so that they could go and get provisions, he said to them, *'You give them something to eat.'*

You give them something to eat! He doesn't say, "Don't worry, I will feed them." He doesn't say, "I am the bread of life," as he does in the Gospel of John. He says, 'You *give them something to eat.'*

There's an ancient monastic teaching about four levels

of meaning in Scripture. The first is the literal or historical meaning: Even though it may not always be factually accurate from the point of history or science, every piece of Scripture still has some historical context. Then there is a symbolic or allegorical meaning to each piece of Scripture. We don't just rest on what happened; we go on to what it *means*, the moral of the story. And then there is the moral meaning, sometimes called the tropological meaning. Every piece of Scripture also acts as a kind of superego, a moral compass giving us direction, some exhortation to upright living and just action. Another great liturgist (and one of the architects of the *Novus Ordo*), Cipriano Vagaggini, used this same schema in regard to the sacraments of the Church as well, teaching that each of the sacraments too carries these various levels of meaning. So for the Eucharist its historical context of course is the Last Supper; its symbolic meaning is both Jesus' self-sacrifice and the communion of all the recipients both with Christ and with each other. But Fr. Vagaggini goes on to refer to the Eucharist as also being a "moral sign obligating." By our reception of Holy Communion, we are pledging, obligating ourselves to a way of life.

In a similar vein Nathan Mitchell refers to an "ethics of eucharist," even an "economics of eucharist" that, he says, "we are not free to ignore." *'You give them something to eat.'* Along with our idea of Eucharist being "just enough for the day," Mitchell says that "if we come away from the table feeling fat, full, content, and satisfied—if we come away purring like cats, licking the last drop of cream from our whiskers—then we've missed the point. Because the point of the eucharistic meal is not to leave the table sleek, sassy, and satisfied." No, he says, the point is to leave hungry, troubled, dissatisfied: "The point is to leave with a burr under the saddle, with a tickle in the throat, with a heart broken by the passion of God."

What is that burr under the saddle? What is that tickle in the throat? It's the spur to now do as Jesus did, to have compassion on the crowds as Jesus did, because they were like sheep without a shepherd. As Jesus exhorts his disciples after washing their feet on Holy Thursday, *'that you also should do.'*[4]

Every sacrament is a moral sign obligating; every sacrament obliges us to a way of life, to some kind of moral action. With our reception of the Eucharist, we commit ourselves to the moral action of washing feet, to being servants. *'The greatest among you will be your servant.'*[5] As Pope Benedict pointed out in his very first encyclical, *Deus Caritas Est*, in the early days of the Church, as it spread throughout the world, the exercise of charity became established as one of its essential activities *along with* the administration of the sacraments and the proclamation of the word: "Love for widows and orphans, prisoners, and the sick and needy of every kind, is as essential as the ministry of the sacraments and preaching of the Gospel. The Church cannot neglect the service of charity *any more than she can neglect the Sacraments and the Word.*" There is an intrinsic inescapable bond between Eucharist and our life of service and self-giving. Benedict refers to Tertullian, who related how the pagans were struck by the Christians' concern for the needy of every sort; and Ignatius of Antioch who described the Church of Rome as "presiding in charity (agape)" through its charitable activity; and Justin Martyr, who in speaking of the Christians' celebration of Sunday, also mentions their charitable activity, which he links to the Eucharist. This of course flows from Jesus' teaching that the greatest commandment is twofold, love of God and love of neighbor.

---

[4] Jn 13:15.
[5] Mt 23:11.

☙

Now let's take a step backward in the rite itself because another of those multivalent meanings of the Eucharist that often gets neglected is the vital indissoluble link between the Word and the Sacrament, which are always inseparable in liturgical spirituality. (The reformed rites for all the sacraments in the Catholic Church exhort that Scripture always be read as part of administering and celebrating every sacrament. Even when bringing Communion to the sick, the minister is supposed to read the gospel of the day with the recipient.)

Going back to the tension between the table and the altar, reflect for a moment on this image from *Dei Verbum*, the Vatican II document on the Sacred Scripture. "The Church has always venerated the divine Scriptures *as she venerates the Body of the Lord*, in so far as she never ceases, particularly in the Sacred Liturgy, to partake of the Bread of Life and to offer it to the faithful from *the one table of the Word of God and the Body of Christ*" (emphases mine).

The one Table! I once heard a young priest railing from the pulpit against the use of the word "table" to refer to the altar. Perhaps he had not read *Dei Verbum* or perhaps, if he did, he did not agree with its teaching. We need to chew on and consume the words and works of Jesus as much as on the consecrated bread and wine. This is why we speak of "breaking open the Scriptures" as we would a loaf of bread. "As once you did for your disciples, now open the Scriptures for us and break the bread," says the Eucharistic Prayer for Various Needs and Occasions. And Saint Jerome too wrote that eating Christ's flesh and drinking his blood certainly means the mystery of the Eucharist. "However," he says, "his true body and blood are also the Word of the Scriptures and its doctrine." And please let's not forget that according to *Sacrosanctum Concilium*, the document on the reformed liturgy, the first to be issued at the Second Vatican Council, this too is a Real Presence of Christ—"when the Word is proclaimed."

There's a beautiful choreography in the Catholic liturgy, especially evidenced in those rare churches where the assembly actually moves at the conclusion of the Liturgy of the Word to gather in a different space around the altar for the Liturgy of the Eucharist. The point is, and the choreography embodies this, that the Word always demands a response. Now that we have heard the Word and have been challenged by it, we are summoned to do something. "Are you ready? Are you willing?"

The response asked of us is twofold. First of all, we go from the Table of the Word to the Table of the Eucharist. Second, though it is not always practiced this way, the liturgical documents are very clear that the bread and wine are not to be on the altar from the beginning but are instead meant to be presented by members of the assembly. Why is that? Because before the bread and wine become the Real Presence of Christ, they are meant to be the real presence of *us*, symbolic of our lives and our loves, our work and our play, our joys and our sorrows that we are offering. "Are you ready, in response to the Word, as a response to the summons of the gospel of Jesus, to lay your life down on the altar?" That too is a real presence and a sacrifice. And that's what gets lifted up. And accepted. And consecrated (transubstantiated)—our lives and loves, our work and our play, our joys and sorrows. Us.

We get lifted up. Our lives get lifted up. And accepted. And consecrated. And then broken . . .

Another of those little understated moments in the liturgy is called the fraction rite, the breaking of the consecrated bread (and the distribution of the consecrated wine in various chalices if Communion is offered under both species). It's very clear that the priest-presider is supposed to make sure that this little gesture, the cracking open of this loaf of bread, is supposed to be seen by the assembly as they are singing the *Agnus Dei,* the Lamb of God. It recalls the lambs being slaughtered for the Passover feast in the Gospel of John as Jesus is being put to death, and as the bread is broken, we sing the *Agnus Dei,* "Lamb of God . . . have mercy on us." Our lives, our loves laid on the altar and lifted up, conse-crated like the Eucharistic bread, are now broken open and passed out; like the wine that has been crushed like grapes, so our joys and hopes, our grief and anguish, are now poured out. St. Lawrence the deacon and martyr who had given his whole life over in service of the poor, after he was tortured on the grill, just before he died, is reported to have said, "It is finished. Take and eat." He knew he had become Eucha-rist. And there's an amazing famous quote from Ignatius of Antioch as he is facing his death by martyrdom, being fed to lions: "I am Christ's wheat," he writes, "and the teeth of the beasts will grind me into Christ's pure bread." He too knew that he was becoming Eucharist.

And then we get it all back again to consume, to eat and drink. But now it has all—our lives and loves, our work and our play, our joys and hopes, our grief and anguish—been brought into right relationship with God, transformed in the form of bread and wine that has been transubstantiated. Augustine is very clear in stating, "At the altar you receive what you are."

∽

I skipped over two things. First of all, there is a fourth level of meaning to both each Scripture reading and each Sacrament—the mystical meaning (sometimes referred to as the anagogical meaning). And second, that mystical meaning is best conveyed by another micro-rite in the Liturgy of the Eucharist, a prayer that the priest says when adding a drop of water into the wine as the gifts are being prepared, a prayer that does not even have to be said out loud, but that is so powerful, perhaps all the more powerful because of its semi-secret nature. "By the mystery of this water and wine, may we come to share in the divinity of Christ who humbled himself to share in our humanity." If mysticism is about some kind of direct experience of God, "being touched by God in a way that's beyond words, imagination and feeling," as the Carmelite mystical writer Ruth Burrows described it, then this is surely the mystical meaning of this sacrament. What could be more direct than that, the ultimate goal of our participation in the Eucharistic feast—to share in the divinity of Christ?

Now, to be clear, there is a whole lot of dying that has to go on before we can actualize our sharing in the divinity of Christ—dying to our false self, dying to our selfishness, dying to our individuality so as to become a person, as well as giving ourselves over in service to the world around us, being the presence of Christ, doing as Jesus did, washing the feet of each other, of the poor, of the marginalized and even of Mother Nature herself, caring for our planet home and all God's creatures great and small. But the promise remains: If we do so, we can come to share the divinity of Christ through our participation not just in this meal, but in his way of life.

This is a little piece of creation, a little bit of matter, bread and wine, that was the symbol of my life laid on the altar, and that has now been brought into right relationship with God. I now get it back, and I'm asked to consume it. And at that moment I become a tabernacle because, if I ever doubted it before, I have the Real Presence of Christ inside of me. If we're going to take the Real Presence of Christ in the Eucharist seriously, let's take it all the way. I now become the very presence of Christ. I walk out of the doors of the church a monstrance. More important, hopefully I too through my sharing in this meal am starting to be changed permanently into what I have received, and do what Jesus did, and even greater things.[6]

The Eucharist is a sacrificial meal. Not just bread and wine, it becomes body and blood; and not just body and blood but broken body and spilled blood. Before we can reign with Jesus we must die with him, as he did. This fraction, this breaking, is a prophecy, about what this sign will be obligating us to— to be broken and poured out. When we say AMEN! we are committing ourselves to a way of life, which is the poverty, the spiritual poverty of the gospel of Jesus. We may not die on a Calvary, but we are called to die constantly by emptying ourselves in sometimes very small ways, service, patience, kindness, emptying ourselves often simply of our "self-will run riot," emptying ourselves completely, content with the grace of God. Just as the bread gets broken at the altar, just as the wine gets poured out, so we walk out the doors of the church, we who have become the Body of Christ and have been given enough food for the journey, to be broken and poured out for the sake of those whom we love—and those whom we don't.

Of course we need to add, and this is something that was perhaps not emphasized enough in the past, it's not just broken body and spilled blood: The Eucharist is the glorified resurrected body of Christ. And *if we have died with him, we*

---

[6] Cf. Jn 14:12.

will also live with him. If we endure, we will also reign.[7]

There is another part of the Mass that is commonly practiced that is actually not an official part of the Mass: the closing hymn. Believe it or not, a so-called closing hymn is not even listed in the official rubrics of the liturgy. The official formula of the Mass ends very abruptly, with the words "The Mass is ended: Go in peace!" There are different formulas allowed for that: "Go in the peace of Christ. Go in peace to love and serve the Lord. Go in peace glorifying the Lord by your life." But the operative word there is still and always GO!

I am not one to change the words of the Church's liturgy cavalierly, nor do I get too scrupulous about it. But I do tend to squirm when a priest will change that formula to something like, "This Mass is ended; have a nice day!" or anything that neglects that most poignant word—GO! The most important word there is GO!

As the English mystical writer Caryll Houselander wrote, what we are asked to do is to become Christs: "When we are changed into Him as the bread into the Host, then with His power we can follow His example." If I were going to improvise a formula to end the liturgy it would be something like this: "The Mass is ended—now, you go and give them something to eat."

---

[7] 2 Tim 2:11–12.

4

A Body You Have
Prepared for Me

On the Grace of Carnality

I once took part in an interfaith pilgrimage to the Holy Land.
It was mostly Jews and Christians, with one Sufi thrown
in the mix. The whole idea was to visit each other's sacred
spots and to try to learn from each other about our various
traditions. We spent the majority of the trip in the south,
near Jerusalem, and then we went up north, mostly visiting
Christian spots. Our first stop up north was in Nazareth,
and on our first morning we all piled into the Basilica of the
Annunciation. It had very modern architecture and for being
such a popular pilgrimage spot, it was a lot less touristy than
I thought it would be.

One of the features of the place is that there are plaques
in honor of Mary all over the walls in the plaza and in the
basilica itself, from countries all over the world. Once we
were inside I happened to be walking with my friend Rabbi
Paula, who was one of the co-leaders of the trip, and at one
point we were standing in front of the plaque from Portugal

that carried the title "Mary Ark of the Covenant." And Rabbi Paula looked at me oddly and said, "What does *that* mean?" The Ark of the Covenant of course was the most sacred object of the Israelites, a wooden chest adorned with gold that contained the tablets of the Mosaic Law as recorded in the Book of Exodus and the First Book of Kings.[1] Obviously this is something very important to the Jewish tradition—and especially to a rabbi!—and here I was, having to explain to her how and why we had co-opted such a revered term for Mary the mother of Jesus.

And so I launched into it as best I could and, if I recall correctly, rather fast and furiously, the words just tumbling out of my mouth . . . how I understood that we believe that there is an aspect of God that we call the Word, and that Word is the very principle of intelligence and intentionality in the universe; and as St. John explains it in his gospel, that Word is not only *with* God, but that Word *is* God, like the Word that God spoke and all things came into being, as the Psalmist says, or the Wisdom that was at play at God's side all the while.[2] That "Word" is what lies before all specific laws or dogmas, even before the Law as articulated in the Torah and the Ten Commandments, the covenant, like the *tao* that the classic Chinese book of mystical poetry the Tao te Ching says is before all virtues; and that Word is always being spoken to us, transmitted to us, but we can't hear it in the sense of fully receive it—it's in *sighs too deep for words,*[3] as St. Paul says, or maybe like the OM that the Indian tradition believes hums beneath all created things.

But we believe that Mary was a human being so pure, so

---

[1] Ex 37:1–9, 40:20; 1 Kgs 8:9.
[2] Ps 33:9; Pr 8:30.
[3] Rom 8:26.

receptive, that she was able to fully receive that Word, so much so that *it became something in her*; it took root like a seed in the garden of her womb; it took flesh in her, it became a baby, and she named that baby Jesus, in whom we believe the fullness of divinity dwelt bodily because he was that very Word made flesh. And so we believe that this is the *new* covenant, or better, the fulfillment of the covenant: this is what God had intended all along, for there to be no separation between heaven and earth, that we would share in divinity through, with, and in the Word. And so Mary, pregnant with Jesus, is the Ark of this New Covenant, because she is carrying the Word-made-flesh inside her.

There was a gentleman on the trip, a wonderful older man, a little less sophisticated than the rabbi, the minister, the monk, the Sufi, and the rest of the crowd, but totally unintimidated, and he was always saying things that were filled with a kind of innocent wonder. I didn't know it, but he was standing at my shoulder listening to my whole spontaneous breathless discourse, and when I had finished, and Paula and I were standing there absorbing this moving moment, suddenly this guy bursts out and says right into my ear, "You know, I never thought of it like that! So this is kinda where the whole thing got started, huh?" And suddenly I thought to myself, "You know, I actually had never thought of it that way before either. But, ya, you're right. This *is* where it all got started, with Mary receiving the Word so deeply into her heart that it became something in her; actually, it became *someone* in her, in her very body."

᭒

In the Jewish tradition there is a type of literature called *midrash*, which is exegesis, commentary, and interpretation on

Scripture. It's very common in the rabbinic tradition. Often *midrash* explains moral principles and theological concepts, but *midrashim* are also trying to explain the full meaning of the biblical law and find the hidden meanings or new meanings in the Scripture passage. Sometimes it almost seems as if some of the Christian Scriptures started out as simply *midrash* on the Jewish Scriptures. And we are one step removed: We're trying to understand the Christian Scriptures that are trying to explain the Jewish ones. One good example of this is in the Gospel of Luke; it often seems as if the evangelist is doing *midrash* on the Jewish Scriptures.

For example, our naming of Mary the new "Ark of the Covenant" is no accident. It's not very well hidden in Luke's gospel. There's the story of what we call the Visitation,[4] when Mary, pregnant with Jesus, goes to visit her cousin Elizabeth, who is pregnant with John, who will grow up to be the Baptizer. And Elizabeth says, *'At the moment the sound of your greeting met my ear, the infant in my womb leaped for joy.'* Not only is the whole layout of the story strikingly similar to the story of David dancing before the Ark in 2 Samuel[5]; Luke uses the same Greek word—*skirtan*, "dance"—for what John the Baptist is doing in his mother's womb that the ancient Greek translation of the Jewish Scriptures called the Septuagint uses for what David does before the Ark. It's almost as if Luke is purposely using the story of David bringing the Ark of the Covenant into Jerusalem as a literary framing device. So it is actually Luke who is telling us that this is the new law, the new covenant and, as he does throughout the infancy narratives, telling us that this is the fulfillment, as Elizabeth says, of the promises of the Lord. And John is dancing before the

---

[4] Lk 1:39–45.
[5] 2 Sam 6:13–21.

Ark that/who Mary is. So this could be seen as Luke's *midrash* on 2 Samuel.

When we celebrate the feast of the Annunciation, when the angel Gabriel tells Mary, *'you will conceive in your womb and bear a son, and you will name him Jesus,'*[6] the liturgical tradition pairs that story from the Gospel of Luke with a reading from the Letter to the Hebrews, and here's another Christian *midrash*.[7] The author to the Letter to the Hebrews quotes Psalm 40 but actually misquotes it or purposely changes it. Psalm 40 actually says, *Sacrifice and offerings you did not desire, but an open ear.* But Hebrews says instead, *When Christ came into the world, he said, 'Sacrifices and offerings you have not desired, but* a body *you have prepared for me.'* So the ear has become a whole body, or the whole body has become like an open ear—the whole body has become a listening, a receptivity, an availability.

I used to think that "body" here referred to Jesus' body, and of course it does, but it strikes me now that it could just as well refer to Mary's body. Mary, whose whole body was a listening, whose whole body was a receptivity, an open ear— the ear of her body, the ear of her soul, as well as the ear of her heart, as St. Benedict calls it, her spirit. Her whole body was a vessel, not just her mind or her soul, nor some kind of disembodied spirit. Mary's body was a living breathing blood-filled pulsing grounded vessel. Her sacrifice was her whole being, including her body. She became the Ark of the New Covenant, carrying within her the new law.

Psalm 40 tells us, and the author to the Letter to the Hebrews interprets it for us, that as fine as they are, ultimately God does not really want our ritual sacrifices and liturgical

---

[6] Lk 1:26–38.
[7] Heb 10:5–7.

offerings and doesn't need our holocausts offered on the altar. What God really requires of us is what those sacrifices and offerings are supposed to symbolize. What Jesus' ultimate prayer was, in the middle of the Our Father as well as in the garden of Gethsemane, is what God requires: *Behold I have come to do your will.* As Mary says, *'Here am I, the servant of the Lord, let it be with me according to your word.'*[8] An open ear, a body offered up as a spiritual sacrifice, our whole being—body, soul, and spirit available to be a vehicle, a vessel, an instrument.

This is the great turnaround, the extra step that most spiritual traditions are hesitant to take, all the way from classical yoga through Christianity. First of all, the body is a vehicle. The Catechism quotes the famous dictum of the second-century father Tertullian, *Caro cardo salutis es,* "the flesh is the hinge of salvation." Even that much has taken us a long time to accept, and of course classical yoga embraces that, and this is what we learn from it in our spiritual practice. We usually tend to think in the spiritual life that we peel the body off like a banana peel and throw it away (a phrase of the Paulist priest and yogi Tom Ryan that I like so much) so we can be "spiritual." But somehow this whole great story all the way from the Annunciation straight through to the Ascension—with the birth of Jesus, his healings, the transfiguration, and the resurrection—is trying to convey something even more to us. Not only is the body a worthy vehicle, an instrument, a "hinge." It is also the field of transformation; it is that which gets transformed. Like Mary's whole being became the Ark of the New Covenant.

There are many great minds from across the spectrum of thought that back me up on this. Sam Keen, for instance,

---

[8] Lk 1:38.

in his book *To a Dancing God*, complained that neither the Christian culture nor the secular culture, in which he had been jointly nurtured, had ever taught him how to interpret the sacred in the voice of the body and the language of the senses. "In the same measure that Christian theology has failed to help me realize the *carnality* of grace," he wrote, "secular ideology has failed to provide me categories for understanding the *grace* of carnality." Religious people, Christians but not only, are much more accustomed to an emphasis on the spiritual realm and tend to get uncomfortable with too much specific emphasis on the body. Christopher West, who was one of the great disseminators of the thought of John Paul II, says it's because of this that we constantly swing back and forth between angel-ism, prudishness, rigorism, and repression, on the one hand, all the way to indulgence and indecency, on the other. The solution is never to swing from one end of the pendulum to the other, but to find the integration in right relationship, an *integral* relationship, the unity of body and soul, even the unity of spirituality and sexuality.

In his seminal and brilliant essay "The Body and the Earth," the great American novelist, poet, essayist, farmer, and social critic Wendell Berry uses similar language when he refers to "the isolation of the body." He says that at some point we began to assume that "the life of the body should be the business of grocers and medical doctors who don't have to take any interest in the spirit; and the life of the spirit should be the domain of churches who would have at best only a negative interest in the body." But if the soul lives by denying the body, first of all its relation to the world eventually grows too superficial to cope with the world in any meaningful way, and we shouldn't be surprised to find out that spiritual values have ceased to carry any weight or any authority. If the soul lives by denying the body, we shouldn't wonder why our spiritual values lack vigor or power or purpose in the world. It's not possible to devalue the body and value the soul!

Now why that kind of dualism ought to be a huge surprise for the Christian is that our whole spirituality is based on the fact that God—in the Person of the Word—became flesh! So how could the flesh be intrinsically evil if Christians claim that God did it the wonderful compliment of taking it on? Again, think of Jesus and the marvelous events in his life and ministry. First of all, that he spent a good deal of time healing people's bodies as well as feeding them. But then before his death he is transfigured in the sight of his apostles on Mount Tabor, his very flesh sharing in the transforming power of divinity. (The Gospel of Mark tells us that even his robe was whiter than any fuller could dye it.) And of course, the story doesn't end with Jesus' death but the resurrection, *bodily* resurrection. As Wendell Berry adds, "Nothing could be more absurd than to despise the body and yet yearn for resurrection!"

I always like to add the caveat for people who have a hard time believing in the reality of the resurrection, please don't get caught up in the facts as if the Gospels were a science book or a history book. Don't miss the point of the story, the moral of the myth: The Gospels are teaching us that the body is not left behind to rot; even the body shares in the glory. Granted the stories also tell us it is some kind of glorified body post-resurrection that can walk through walls and still eat fish, but the body is central there. (Remember the apostle Thomas asking to touch the holes in Jesus' hands and his side.) And finally, also, the ascension forty days after the resurrection. Again, please don't get caught up in the science and the history and miss the point. Our tradition is telling us that even in the end there is some kind of body; even at the very end the flesh is not discarded, not peeled off, but changed in some marvelous way.

Who made bold new moves on this was Pope John Paul II in his *Theology of the Body*, which I think is under-appreciated by liberals. You may have heard it said that Bach's music, for instance, is theology in music. In a similar vein, Pope John Paul went on to speak not only of a theology *of* the body, but the *body as a theology* if we read it correctly, which of course is not always the case. Christopher West had one of the greatest book titles of all time about all this called *Naked without Shame*. He insists that "it is through our bodily senses and the 'stuff' of the material world that we most intimately encounter God." For this reason, the human body itself is in some sense sacramental, in the broader more ancient sense of the word "sacrament": It is a sign that makes visible the invisible mystery of God. "The body is the primordial and pre-eminent sign of the ultimate spiritual reality," West writes. So we can study the body as a theology, as a sacrament, as a sign of the ultimate spiritual reality, the divine mystery.

I have noticed even among enlightened spiritual traditions how often it is said that "we are not our bodies." I am not sure that is completely accurate, or at least it presents us with a slippery slope toward a whole new kind of dualism. This to me is where the incarnational theology of Christianity really comes to the fore—or ought to. Again Sam Keen warns us that we have to be careful of being seduced by the dualism implicit in the kind of language that encourages us to speak of "having a body," as if the possessor and the possessed were two different entities. All human knowledge, all human value and aspiration are stamped with the mark of the body. Our body is our bridge to and model of the world; therefore, *how we are in our body so will we be in the world*. This is very important! Because as I trust or mistrust the rhythm of my body, so I trust or mistrust my total world. If we lose the self, we lose the other; if we lose the body, we lose the world. That's the danger of not loving one's body. "Love of both neighbor and cosmos rests upon love of self."

The other side of this "enlightened dualism" is represented by someone like the Black writer Ta-Nehisi Coates. "I believed, and still do, that our bodies are ourselves," he says, "and my soul is the voltage conducted through neurons and nerves, and that my spirit is my flesh." This was quoted in a marvelous collection called *Black Liturgies* by Cole Arthur Riley, who is also the author of another best-selling book called *This Here Flesh*. Is there something particularly about Black people in America that doesn't want to hear the message that "you are not your body"? It is a disregard for the body that "justifies," if you will, abuse of other people's bodies, things such as slavery, for instance, as well as capital punishment.

This of course is not high theology, what I like to think of as "trickle down theology." No, this is theology from the ground up, from the flesh up, incarnate, the body as a theology, even a deconstruction and a reconstruction of theology.

To put it simply, our body can either be an enemy or a friend, a means and a hinge or a burden. I say, make it your friend! And somehow *this* is the fulfillment of the promise that started out with the promise to Abraham. As Paul says in 1 Corinthians, a little phrase that haunted Teilhard de Chardin, *so that God may be all in all.* Paul is speaking here of the resurrection and a little later about physical death, so do not over-spiritualize this. Just as earlier in the same letter when he writes to the Corinthians, *The body is meant . . . for the Lord and the Lord for the body . . .* and *do you not know your bodies are members of Christ?* And *your bodies are a temple of the Holy Spirit within you . . .* and so *glorify God in your body.*[9] Again, let's not over-spiritualize this either: This is the section of Paul's Letter to the Corinthians about gluttony and fornication; he really means the flesh. Don't indulge in those things because *this* instead is what your glorious human body is meant for, to be a temple of the Holy Spirit. One of my favorite lines is in the Letter to the Romans, chapter 12, when he urges his readers to *offer your bodies as living sacrifices, holy and acceptable, to God, your spiritual worship.*[10]

So it's not just about Mary. Jesus will say in reference to his own mother, *'Blessed are* all those *who hear the word of God and keep it.'*[11] All of us become Arks of the Covenant if we but stake our claim on this promise, that *God will be all in all* in us if we offer even *our bodies as spiritual sacrifices*, though not something to be burned up and destroyed, but something to be transformed into a vessel and then transfigured, sharing in the promise of the resurrection if we but offer ourselves up for that Word to take root in the ground of our very being. As the twelfth-century Cistercian abbot and philosopher Isaac of Stella wrote, "Every Christian is also believed to be bride of God's Word, a mother of Christ, . . . at once virginal and fruitful."

☙

It may seem like a bit of a leap, but all this is why I love the practice of yoga and meditation. (I mean "meditation" in the Asian sense here, training the senses and stilling the mind with an aim toward one-pointed concentration.) Growing up a Catholic, I had the impression that going to church meant leaving your body at the door. You covered as much

---

[9] 1 Cor 5:12–20.
[10] Rom 12:1.
[11] Lk 11:28.

of your body as possible (women in those days even had to cover their heads), and it was all celebrated "from the cheeks up." Everything was going on in my mind, though occasionally the heart would kick in too. I learned to meditate as an adult, mainly from Buddhism and from the yoga tradition of India, the art of "training the senses and stilling the mind." And in both of those cases the first thing you learn is how to sit properly. That simple. The Buddhists are brilliant at the mechanics of mapping out the inscape of the mind, making the interior journey, but of primary importance is that one solid unmoving sitting position during the period of meditation, committing for a length of time to the poverty of this certain posture. We come to the mind through the body. And then, to use the words of another ancient Eastern Christian writer, Theophan the Recluse, we "put our mind in our heart."

That is where the yoga tradition has been incomparably valuable to me, especially when I read this one simple line: "The reason we do these *asanas* [stretching and strengthening poses] is so that we can sit in meditation longer." Brilliant. I remember sitting for the first time in something like what is called the "half-lotus position" on my *zafu* (sitting cushion) on the floor and thinking to myself very clearly, "This is where it's happening. Right here. In this body. This is my church, my temple, this is my place of encounter with God, in this body." I remembered Saint Paul's words, *The body is meant for the Lord and the Lord for the body,* and *Do you not know your bodies are members of Christ? And your bodies are a temple of the Holy Spirit within you so glorify God in your body.*[12] And I carry that temple with me wherever I go.

And speaking of Mary, one of my mentors, the one who initiated me into my own serious yoga practice, suggested

---

[12] 1 Cor 5:12–20.

that this is what the ancient yogis of India were trying to ac-complish in their own way with their practice, to allow the whole person—spirit, soul, and body—to become a vessel of divinity. An open ear, a body offered up as a spiritual sacri-fice, our whole being body, soul, and spirit available to be a vehicle, a vessel, an instrument, a receptacle for the Word to take root and become something in me, even in my very body.

The leap from this to being a "Christian yogi" is no leap at all.

℘

I remember in a discussion I had once with a Buddhist monk who said that for Buddhist monks the main practice was meditation, *zazen* in his tradition, emptying the mind and sitting. Whereas, this monk said, "The main practice of you Christian monks seems to be chanting the psalms." And I said, "No, I think our main practice is actually *listening*, not chanting." We even only chant the psalms so that we can *hear* them. We're singing them to each other, for each other, flinging them across the choir to each other so that we can hear them.

Now, I am quite devoted to silent meditation as well, but I think that even that practice is about something more. As the founder of my monastic tradition, Saint Romuald, taught, "Empty yourself completely and sit waiting." So, the listening presupposes a certain silence, but when we empty ourselves, we wait; while we meditate, we listen, but "listening" in the absolute broadest sense of the word, listening as a symbol of my whole person being a receptivity, like the receptivity of a fruitful virginal womb. Hence, the first word of the Prologue to St. Benedict's Rule for monks is, *Obsculta!* "Listen!"

But it's a special kind of listening. St. Benedict goes on,

Incline the ears of your heart. It's that same heart that Benedict tells us at the end of the Prologue to his Rule that we have to prepare along with our *bodies for the battle of holy obedience to his instructions* (in other words, the Word); and then as *we run on the path of God's commandments* (again, the Word), when they really take root in us, those same hearts *will overflow with the inexpressible delight of love.* And I think it's that inexpressible delight of love that is exactly the Word made flesh, the exuberance that is the dynamic behind creation, now happening in us. And the silence becomes an outward sign of our whole-bodied availability and receptivity.

Therefore, silence ought to be the fundamental condition of our heart, maybe even of our bodies. We empty ourselves, and sit, waiting. It is for this that a body has been prepared for us, so that the Word would make a home in our heart, so that our whole being—body, soul, and spirit—would become a receptivity, and that the Word would take flesh and become incarnate in us too, and we once again and continually give birth to Christ in the world.

☙

People are often surprised to find out how much reverence Muslims have for Jesus' mother Mary, and to discover that she is mentioned more times in the Qur'an than in the New Testament. Muslims would not maintain in the same way that we do that Jesus was God incarnate. And yet I came across the writings of someone from a mystical branch of Islam, the folksinger turned Sufi teacher Reshad Feild, who got very close. His poetic explanation of Mary is that she was chosen to bear Jesus because she kept her purity intact. And those who know this "understand that to be pure means to be completely adaptable, to flow with each moment, to be like a running stream cascading from the waters of life itself."

"The eternal messenger is always within," he wrote, "waiting to unfold in the moment through the Word, and one day when Mary is recognized again, there will be a reappearance of the Christ, manifested in the outer world."

We too could pray, with Jesus, with Mary:

> O God, sacrifices and offerings you have not
>   desired,
> but a body you have prepared for me.
> May my whole body be like an open ear,
> a listening, a receptivity, an availability.
> Be it done to me, in me, according to your
>   Word.

5

The Still Small Voice

On Listening to the Silence

Let's return to that intriguing short account about the prophet Elijah in the First Book of Kings. He is at this moment running for his life from the wicked Queen Jezebel who wants him dead because he has slain the prophets of Baal. (Jezebel was married to King Ahab of Israel and had convinced Ahab to turn his back on the god of Israel and worship her god Baal instead.) So, Elijah first flees a day's journey into the wilderness, sits down by a broom tree and prays for death. But instead of dying, he is given to eat and drink by an angel. Strengthened by that nourishment, he gets up and walks forty days to Mount Horeb where he finds a cave. A voice then asks him, "What are you doing here, Elijah?" And Elijah explains that the Israelites have forsaken the covenant, and his own life is in danger because he has such zeal for the Lord of hosts. He is then told to stand in front of the mountain, because the Lord is about to pass by.

Now there was a great wind, so strong that it was splitting mountains and breaking rocks in pieces before the Lord, but the Lord was not in the wind; and after the wind an earthquake, but the Lord was not in the earthquake; and after the earthquake a fire, but the Lord was not in the fire; and after the fire a sound of sheer silence. When Elijah heard it, he wrapped his face in his mantle and went out and stood at the entrance of the cave.[1]

I was doing music for a silent retreat some years ago, which in and of itself actually caused some consternation for a few of the retreatants. "How can you have music at a silent retreat?!" they protested. The retreat leader was Sr. Ishpriya, an English Sister of the Sacred Heart, who had lived in India for many years studying with swamis, particularly with the highly respected Swami Chidananda at the Divine Light Society in Rishikesh, who was a friend of Abhishiktananda, as was she. She reminded me a lot of Bede Griffiths in that she was dressed in the orange robes of a *sannyasini*, a woman renunciate, and yet when she opened her mouth it was a very polished British accent that came out, and you knew that she was a very well-educated, refined woman. Ishpriya used this reading as the opening talk for this silent retreat, and when she got to the end of the reading she said, "Now of course God *was* in the wind, the earthquake and the fire too, you know!"

There are various poetic translations of those culminating words, the "sound of sheer silence." Sometimes it is rendered "a whispering sound." It's very popular to refer to it also as the "still small voice," as in the well-known English hymn: "Speak through the earthquake, wind, and fire, / O still small voice of calm!" But "the sound of sheer silence" or a "thin silence" is most accurate.

---

[1] 1 Kings 19:11–13.

❧

On one of my trips to India I wound up being almost crippled from what I thought was an injury to my hip but was in reality the recurrence of a bulging disk in my back that was pinching a nerve. I was in so much pain that my brothers and sisters at our ashram, Shantivanam, sent me away for a week in an Ayurvedic hospital in the nearby city of Trichy. My anecdotes about my stay there are a whole other story, but aside from the discomfort of the treatments themselves, it wound up being a wonderful solitary silent retreat since I was in a private room, barely anyone on the staff spoke English, and I rarely saw the few that did.

I only had a few books with me, just a novel I was reading at the time, my Bible, and a copy of the Upanishads. The Upanishads are some of the sacred writings of India. Briefly put, they are esoteric writings that are attached to the end of the larger scriptures known as the Vedas. The distinctive feature of the Upanishads is that they don't deal with calling out to gods and goddesses "out there" or with hymns or sacrifice or ritual. They are devoted to the interior way, the way of meditation, finding the Divine in the *guhā*, the cave of the heart. This interior way is of course explicated in many of our own Christian mystical texts, but there is something special about the way the Upanishads speak about it that is very dear to me, as it was to the folks who have gone before me and inspired my interest in Asian spirituality, including the same Abhishiktananda and Bede Griffiths.

What was interesting about having just the Upanishads and the Bible (mainly to read the psalms and the Gospels) was being able to juxtapose the two, one as an expression of the inner and the other as an expression of the outer because, all things being equal, our own Scriptures don't necessarily speak much about the interior way in an explicit fashion. It's more hidden, perhaps just under the surface. I want to rush in to say there is of course a very strong (though surprisingly little-known) contemplative tradition in Christianity. We might recall the yin-yang symbol of Taoism: just as there is a little spot of dark in the light side and vice versa, so there is of course an interior way in the prophetic traditions, as we sometimes refer to Judaism, Christianity, and Islam; just as there is a dot of engagement with the world in the mystical traditions of Asia, such as Hinduism, Taoism, and Buddhism. That being said, what Christianity is generally associated with is the extraverted way of ministry, of service, of God in heaven. This story from Elijah is one of those few places in our Scriptures where we are given a hint, a glimpse into the mystical path.

Equally little known is that there is a tradition in Christianity that speaks of the First Person of the Trinity as the Silence. The idea of the "silence of the Father" appears for example in the patristic era. Ignatius of Antioch wrote, "There is only one God, revealed by Jesus Christ his Son, who is his Word sprung from the silence." Centuries later John of the Cross echoes this when he writes, "The Father spoke one Word, which was his Son, and this Word he always speaks in eternal silence, and in silence must it be heard by the soul." So there we have it: the First Person of the Trinity (the Father) as the Silence. So maybe that is who we are encountering here in this story of Elijah in the cave.

By the Silence though we don't mean just the absence of words or sounds. It is also referring to God beyond all names and forms, what the great thirteenth-century German mystic Meister Eckhart called "the abyss of the godhead," far beyond our comprehension and all our human notions of who and what we think God is. This is similar to the idea of the Divine that we get from the Upanishads that speak of the divine that is *anamarupa*, beyond name and form. Mystics also refer to this fathomless abyss of the godhead as an emptiness, but it's not the emptiness of a void, or of nihilism. (This is why some Christians, even very intelligent ones, don't understand Buddhism, by the way.) It's an emptiness that is a fullness, in Greek a *kenosis* that is a *pleroma*, in Sanskrit it's the *sunyata* (emptiness) that gives birth to the *purna* (wholeness), a paradox not unlike the sound of sheer silence.

This is where I also love the Chinese Taoist tradition whose poetry for this is exquisite and sublime. *The Tao that can be spoken is not the eternal Tao* is how the whole of the principal text, the *Tao te Ching*, begins. A Taoist might also refer to this as the "generative emptiness at the heart of the cosmos," who is also called "the Great Mother." A *generative* emptiness that is the womb of possibility, from which all flows forth— beyond all name and form, the genuine mystery, the Silence.

We could speculate that this is what—or better, this is *who*—Elijah is encountering here in the sound of sheer silence. And yes, Sr. Ishpriya, God *was* in the earthquake, wind, and fire. But—and I think that Ishpriya would agree with me here—that Silence was the *source* of the earthquake, wind, and fire. The generative emptiness was at the heart of the earthquake, wind, and fire. The Silence came before the earthquake, wind, and fire. The earthquake, wind, and fire all come from that generative emptiness.

And by the way, the answer to why you can have music at a silent retreat is that the best of music too flows from that Silence and leads back to it. As the French liturgist and musician Lucien Deiss always said, "The quality of the music you make must be as good as the quality of the silence you break."

What I came to by the end of that week in the Indian hospital, in a way that had never occurred to me before, is wondering if what was described in the Upanishads was similar to what Jesus himself experienced in the solitary days and nights that he spent in the desert and on the mountains when he slipped away to commune with his *abba* in silence and solitude as we so often hear about in the Gospels.

We don't know much about Jesus' way of praying except what he reveals in the gospel when he is teaching his disciples how to pray, for example: *'Whenever you pray, go into your room and shut the door and pray to your Father who is in secret; and your Father who sees in secret will reward you.'*[2] We're taught always to see Jesus prefigured in the Jewish Scriptures, and so to see Moses as a type of Christ, Isaiah's suffering servant as a type of Christ, Jonah and Jeremiah as types of Jesus, whereas Elijah usually gets associated with John the Baptist. How about if we think of Elijah as a prefiguring of Jesus? In a very literal kind of way. I am tempted to insert the story of Elijah on the mountain from 1 Kings into this story from the Gospel of Matthew, for instance.

> After he had fed the people, Jesus made his disciples get into a boat and precede him to the other side, while he dismissed the crowds. After doing so, Jesus went up on the mountain by himself to pray. . . . And he came to a cave where he took shelter. Then the Spirit said to him, "Go outside and stand on the mountain, for your *abba* will be passing by." And there was a great wind, and there was an earthquake, and there was a fire, but his *abba* was not in the wind, the earthquake, or the fire. But after that, there was the sound of sheer silence. When Jesus heard this, he wrapped his face in his mantle and went out and stood at the entrance of the cave.

---

[2] Mt 6:5–6.

This is the part that is always missing for us, what happened to Jesus not only in those lost years of his life from age twelve to thirty, but also in all those unrecorded moments, what he experienced, how he prayed. Maybe *this* is what Jesus experienced, something like what Elijah had experienced. The nineteenth-century English hymn writer John Whittier, who wrote the text of that famous English hymn mentioned above, thought so. The third verse goes like this:

> O Sabbath rest of Galilee!
> O calm of hills above,
> Where Jesus knelt to share with thee
> The silence of eternity,
> Interpreted by love.

The silence of eternity interpreted by love! In his Sabbath rest of Galilee, on the calm of its hills, is this what Jesus experienced, what the hymn writer later calls "the still small voice of calm," the silence of eternity? Is this what Jesus experienced on the mountain, in the desert, in the wilderness, the Divine One beyond all names and forms of the Upanishads? The God of the sound of sheer silence, who Saint Gregory of Nyssa and Saint John of the Cross say is the God who dwells in darkness—a holy darkness—rather than in light the more we approach the summit of the mountain? I guess we won't ever really know exactly what Jesus did, how he prayed, but we do know that Jesus himself said to the Samaritan woman, *'The hour is coming, and is now here, when you will worship the Father neither on this mountain nor in Jerusalem . . . when true worshippers will worship the Father in spirit and truth'* because *'God is Spirit and those who worship him must worship in spirit and in truth.'*[3]

---

[3] Jn 4:21–24.

Perhaps we could say that this is where Jesus really dwelt in his solitary moments, in the cave of his own heart, the *guhā*, and in that cave of his heart what reigned was that gentle breeze, the sound of sheer silence, the still small voice of calm. But it wasn't just a psychological tool or even a self-powered trance-like state, nor an anonymous faceless force, but what the hymn writer calls "the silence of eternity interpreted by love," a deep-seated knowledge that this silence, this gentle breeze that was the ground of his own being and consciousness was also in some marvelous way intentional and loving and benevolent—like an *abba*, a loving generous parent. And that is Jesus' gift to the world, to invite others to trust the benevolence that is both the source of the universe and the ground of their own being and consciousness, too. The silence of eternity interpreted by love.

In our daily lives and in our place in the world and history, this may be one of the specific gifts that Christians have to offer—our own experience of this benevolent God of Jesus. And even more those in the contemplative tradition are to lead others too to this experience of God in the cave of the heart, the loving silence of eternity that is the ground of being and depth of the soul. Especially in a society driven wild by consumerism and consumption and a world gone mad with aggression and vengeance, this is what we need, this is what the world needs, and this is what we need to be.

This is the last most famous verse of that hymn:

> Breathe through the hearts of our desire
> Thy coolness and thy balm;
> Let sense be dumb, let flesh retire;
> Speak through the earthquake, wind and fire,
> O still small voice of calm.

John Main, the inspirer of the World Community for Christian Meditation, often referred to the silence that is already in us, the silence at the core of our own being. Of course, he is speaking of silent meditation and that's what we hope to find and realize, the silent depth within us. When Jesus tells us that we should fast and pray and give alms in secret, and that our Father who sees in secret will see us, it's that place he is referring to, a point in us that is also a fathomless abyss, a generative emptiness, a kenosis that is a fullness. It may be a very deep dig, but the silence is inside you; it's the core of our being. It is that from which you and I come forth, the generative emptiness, beyond name and form, at the heart of the cosmos.

When the spiritual writer Martin Laird gave us a retreat some years ago, one of the pearls of wisdom he said forms part of the litany I use to prepare myself for meditation: "Greet everything with stillness." And he used the image of a fog bank rolling in, or like silk, and he said we ought to wrap every thought in the silk of that silence. The silk of silence that is at the heart of our being, the point of our union with God who is our generative source, who is the Silence, beyond name and form, at the heart of our being.

∽

One last thought on this, that I got from Robert Cardinal Sarah in his book *The Power of Silence*. Remember that before this event Elijah is running scared from the wicked Queen Jezebel. Well, after the theophany in the sound of sheer silence, Elijah is asked the same thing he was asked before the theophany: *Then there came a voice to Elijah that said, 'What are you doing here, Elijah?'* That question is all important. Sure enough, the next thing Elijah does after this experience of meeting God in the sound of sheer silence is to go back down the mountain, continue with his prophetic mission, and throw his mantle over Elisha. He regains courage and then passes the experience on. Out of his experience, as the Tibetan Buddhists say about monks after their three-year solitary retreat, he comes back to the world "with bliss-bestowing hands," with that still small voice of calm enabling him to conquer his fear and do what he is being called to do.

Cardinal Sarah comments that one day, "beyond the invasive noise that is perversely interwoven in so many lives," it will be important to listen once again to that "still small voice," the voice that is going to ask *us*, "What are you doing *here?*" A lot of people who come to our hermitage for retreat hit that point when the outer and inner noise dies down, a moment when they reflect on their lives for the first time in a while and a little voice says to them, "What are you doing with your life?" As a matter of fact, I met a man once who told me that he came for a retreat at our place once intending to stay for three days, but he left after the second day because, he told me, "I knew if I stayed one more day, I would change my entire life. And I wasn't willing to do that."

It doesn't end in the experience of the silence of God in the cave of the heart; rather, everything begins there. This is very important. "The silence of eternity" is always "interpreted by love," Jesus' love for his *abba* as well as his compassion for the crowds who were *like sheep without a shepherd*.[4] Every time we see Jesus alone in prayer in the Gospels it's always followed by some manifestation of his power to save or feed or heal with his bliss-bestowing hands. Just before that event in Matthew 14 we heard that the crowds were following Jesus to his deserted place. He doesn't send them away and tell them

---

[4] Mt 9:36.

that he's taking a retreat day; he cures them and then he feeds them. And he does the same thing again in very next chapter. And right after that we hear about Jesus' transfiguration, after which he again immediately comes down the mountain and he heals an epileptic.

The interior way doesn't leave out the extraverted way, the way of ministry and mission and work in the world. That still small voice, that is often overlooked in our discernments, then becomes the inspiration and the source of our work in the world. There's a commission that comes after the theophany. Equally important, the authentic commission may come *only* after the theophany, after the experience of God in silence; the full understanding of the commission may only come in the silent holy darkness where God is. "God always speaks this word in eternal silence, and in silence must it be heard by the soul."

But be assured: from out of the silence there will be a call.

We could hope for this grace: to know the Silence that is our source, the still small voice of calm that gives us courage to face the day, to face the troubles in our lives. The silence in which our commission lies. And then to be able to greet everything with that stillness, with that peace, and draw from, live from, the well of silent grace that is at the heart of our being.

6

Here I Am,
for You Called Me

On Vocation

There's a charming story told in the Book of Samuel about the call of the prophet of the same name when he was yet a boy and ministering to the Lord under the priest Eli at a time when *the word of the Lord was rare,* and *visions were not widespread.*

> Samuel was lying down in the temple of the Lord, where the ark of God was. Then the Lord called, "Samuel! Samuel!" and he said, "Here I am!" and ran to Eli, and said, "Here I am, for you called me." But he said, "I did not call; lie down again." So he went and lay down. The Lord called again, "Samuel!" Samuel got up and went to Eli, and said, "Here I am, for you called me." But he said, I did not call, my son; lie down again." Now Samuel did not yet know the Lord, and the word of the Lord had not yet been revealed to him. The Lord called Samuel again, a third time. And

he got up and went to Eli, and said, "Here I am, for you called me." Then Eli perceived that the Lord was calling the boy. Therefore Eli said to Samuel, "Go, lie down; and if he calls you, you shall say, 'Speak, Lord, for your servant is listening.' " So Samuel went and lay down in his place. Now the Lord came and stood there, calling as before, "Samuel! Samuel!" And Samuel said, "Speak, for your servant is listening."[1]

Before I entered monastic life, I had a very short stint as a seminarian for the diocese of Phoenix in Arizona. When I was going through the interview process for the vocation program, one of the religious women who was on the vocation board explained her approach to me like this. She said, "These young guys come waltzing in here announcing to us that they have a vocation to the priesthood. 'I'm going to be a priest!' they say. And the first thing we tell them," she said, "is 'Slow down, cowboy! *We'll* be the judge of that.' " The idea was, as she explained it to me, that there are three parts to a call, a vocation, any vocation. There is, first of all, the call from God. Then there is the inner call, what we want, what we think we should be doing, what we desire, what gives us life. Equally important to those two, however, is the indispensable call of the community, the call *from* the community. So, you want to be a priest? Fine. But does the community want you to be their priest? Does the church recognize those gifts in you that are necessary for the priesthood?

I usually think of the first two together, the call from God and the inner call, and this story of the call of Samuel is a beautiful example of that. However, my nuance on what the

---

[1] 1 Sam 3:3–10.

good sister said would be that I think the most commonly experienced initial "call" is actually what she named second, what we want to be or dream of being. There is a famous phrase from the late Frederick Buechner that if I have used once I have used a hundred times when speaking to people about vocation. I have it written on the first page of my Bible as well. "The place God calls you is the place where your deep gladness and the world's deep hunger meet." There's a profound truth there.

In another story about a call, at the beginning of the Gospel of John, John the Baptist was standing with two of his disciples, and Jesus walked by.[2] And the Baptizer suddenly exclaimed, *'Look, here is the Lamb of God!'* When the two disciples heard this, they immediately began to follow Jesus. But then something rather dramatic happens. Jesus notices them following him, and he suddenly turns around and says to them, *'What are you looking for?'* What a marvelous question to ask! A great question for us too: What am I looking for?! Because "the place God calls you is the place where your deep gladness and the world's deep hunger meet." What is your deep gladness? What are you looking for? That's where God calls you.

There is a famous phrase of Joseph Campbell that gets bandied about a lot: "Follow your bliss." There is a profound inarguable truth there as well, and at the same time we have to recognize that we may not even really know what authentic bliss is as opposed to fleeting pleasures. Certainly what I thought was bliss at twenty-five years old is a lot different from what I experienced as bliss at forty-five or what I understand bliss to be at sixty-five. And Campbell himself had a more nuanced view of it than a simple one-liner as well.

---

[2] Jn 1:35–39.

In his famous book *The Hero's Journey* he suggests something deeper. "If your bliss is just your fun and your excitement," he writes, then "you're on the wrong track. I mean, you need instruction. Know where your bliss is. And that involves coming down to a deep place in yourself."

The place God calls you, where that bliss resides, is in that deep place. How often do we go deep enough in ourselves to find that place? The call from God is a very mysterious and subtle thing. As John of the Cross taught, God "always speaks in eternal silence, and in silence must it be heard by the soul." How often are we really silent enough to hear that call? Remember too the story of Elijah in the cave: God was not in the earthquake, wind, or fire, but in the sound of sheer silence. How often do we access that inner cave of silence where God speaks in a still small voice? Have we *ever* entered that deeper inner cave of silence where God speaks? It is poignant that the call comes in the night, in the darkness, too, in the holy darkness. And it's notable that Eli doesn't hear the voice that Samuel hears in the night; maybe that's because the call is indeed actually coming from within, from what India calls "the cave of the heart," God speaking directly to Samuel's heart, a still small voice that only he could hear.

In the deep dark silent cave of the heart.

Even here, though, that's just a part of it. Another thing we learn from the story of the call of Samuel is that oftentimes we don't even understand that call unless someone interprets it for us, helps us understand it. As Joseph Campbell says, we need instruction. Someone may even need to tell us that it's God calling, as Eli did for Samuel. That's the role of the community, of mentors and teachers, pointing something out to us that we may not even see, helping us discern and clarify, helping us understand what the Spirit is saying to us.

This call of the community, the call of others, is equally,

vitally important, even indispensable. And of course we aren't speaking only about priesthood and religious life. This concerns every vocation, the need to recognize, call out, nurture, and encourage the gifts of artistry, of athletics, of craftwork, of caregiving, of cooking and sewing, gifts of parenting and mentoring, as well as administration and teaching and leadership.

And then there is still another step, perhaps the hardest one.

There is an excerpt from David Brooks's excellent book *The Road to Character* that I have used for vocation retreats. He's telling the stories of admirable historical figures who answered a summons to leadership, innovation, or service, and he says what we learn from them is that we don't simply *create* our lives; "we are summoned by life." The important answers are not only found *inside* of us; they are also found outside of us, other voices, the situation in which we are embedded. Like Eli instructing Samuel to answer, like John the Baptist pointing out Jesus. This perspective doesn't begin with an autonomous self; it begins with the concrete circumstances in which we are embedded. "This perspective begins with an awareness that the world existed long before you and will last long after you." (As Richard Rohr says, *your life is not about you*! You're a part of something bigger.) And "in the brief span of your life you have been thrown by fate, by history, by chance, by evolution, or by God into a specific place with specific problems and needs." And that place and these people are calling you. "Your job is to figure certain things out: What does this environment need in order to be made whole? What is it that needs repair? What tasks are lying around waiting to be performed?"

And then Brooks references that same Frederick Buechner aphorism in this context: "At what point do my talents and deep gladness meet the world's deep need?"

If I may use another example from my own life, I was being prepared for leadership in our monastic community from my early years as a monk. But to everyone's disappointment (even my own to some extent), after ten years of monastic life I took what we call in our tradition an "exclaustration," that is, I asked permission to live away from the community, which I did then for another ten years. To make a long story short, I could say that at that point in my vocation I had grown disillusioned with Christian Catholic religious life in general, and with Camaldolese Benedictine monastic life in particular. Of course, it was not just about "them," that is, my brother and sister monks and nuns, priests and sisters; it was also about *me*. In that moment I felt as if I had hit a glass ceiling and I wanted to make a step forward spiritually, psychologically, and emotionally (all tied together) that I did not think I was going to be able to make there in community. With the help of good counselors I discerned that I really needed to be out on my own to do that. It was not an easy decision to come to, nor was it an easy transition out, but I was intent on trying the whole enterprise—monasticism, priesthood—in a new way. I really wanted to immerse myself more deeply in Asian spirituality, for one thing, especially the yoga tradition, and also to build a monastic container made out of materials from that forest, as well as to be closer to the People of God and bring light and hope to them through music.

I can safely say that well before the first three years of my exclaustration were up, I was writing to our prior general in Italy saying, "I know that you all think that I am out here re-discerning my vocation. But I think that I have actually *found* my vocation." I could honestly say that my deep gladness—what I loved to do, the unique gifts I had to offer in music and teaching—was meeting a deep hunger in the world. And I had reached the point where I was even willing for the congregation to "kick me out," as it were, if it came to that, if they would not allow me to continue to live in that way and remain in good standing with them, because I was so sure that I was experiencing what Thomas Merton famously called my "true self." After many years of mighty struggle, I was sure I had found my bliss. The congregation, happily, had both the generosity and the creativity to allow me to continue that experiment and kept extending the permission for me to do so in good standing.

As the term of the current prior of my own community was coming to a close, however, there was more and more pressure on me to leave that life I loved and return to community, with the thought that I would, ironically, probably be asked to step in as the new prior. And the call to do so grew more and more persistent, like the hound of heaven, not only from the community, but from the larger congregation as well, then directly from the prior general. I remember two times it even came from someone outside of the immediate community, once from a monk of another community who knew us well who told me that I simply had to go back and be prior; and another time from a friend of the community who is a theology professor. He didn't try to convince me by flattering me and telling me what a great prior I would be. He simply said, "Everybody has to take their turn, Cyprian, and now it's your turn." And with all those voices clamoring for the same thing, I had to assume it was the voice of the Church and the voice of the Spirit. Which went along with something that both one of our elder monks and the prior general himself would say to me at my installation: "Remember, being prior, being a leader, is also an obedience." (At a certain point, I said those same words to my own successor: "Everybody has to take their turn, and I think it's your turn next.")

Along with his notion of the "true self," Thomas Merton

also issued a warning in *No Man Is an Island*: "The deep secrecy of my own being is often hidden from me by my own estimate of what I am," because my idea of what I am is often "falsified by my admiration for what I do." I often wonder how much Merton himself experienced this. And I knew during that phase of my life (I want to say, "at that moment," as if it was just one particular moment) that I was standing at the threshold of a new kind of maturity, or at least another step into spiritual maturity, and that my next step was going to determine everything. I started to discover the difference between self-fulfillment and the true self, meaning I had the sense that somehow if I weren't careful, I could actually become a caricature of my "true self," a whole new kind of false self.

So this call from the community can have a negative as well as a positive side to it, or at least can present us with a challenge. It can call us out of our little world of autonomy into even deeper relationship. Remember Saint Peter: maybe his first joy is going to be following Jesus and being named "the Rock" and being the most trusted disciple. But that initial bliss is going to mature and become something else in him, a call within a call to something more, a stretch, literally. Jesus is going to tell Peter that at the end of his life *'you will stretch out your hands, and someone else will fasten a belt around you and take you where you do not wish to go.'* [3] There's an obedience, a summons to go somewhere, to do something that we might not have chosen to do on our own.

And we simply have to believe that there is another, deeper kind of gladness, perhaps even a bliss, that awaits us then and there too.

There are two little pieces of wisdom that I learned from

---

[3] Jn 21:18.

the Jesuits, who are brilliant at discernment. One is that discernment is ultimately a choice between two goods. After we have gone through what we call the purgative way, when we have rid ourselves of bad habits and freed ourselves somewhat from addictions and compulsivities, then the choices in life are not so much between good and evil; they are between one good and another good. And the second flows right from that: What we are always looking for is not just the good, but the greatest good, the *summum bonum*.

And this is exactly what I was wrestling with. There at fifty-something years old, I was asking myself, "What does a man do now?" By that I don't mean a man as opposed to a woman, I mean a man as opposed to a boy, an adult rather than a child. On the one hand (and I spoke to my best friends about this often), it seemed like a very mature thing to do to take the risk of staying out on my own in this new form of my vocation, which was a way of insecurity and had no clear approbation from my family or the Church, but that felt creative and courageous, and to stay as far away from the institution as possible. On the other hand, was it actually the mature thing instead to do what my father might do, that is (if you'll excuse the sports metaphor), to "step up to the plate" for my family—my monastic family—who really needed me. What was the *greatest* good? Not just for me, but for my place in the world.

So-called self-fulfillment is only a first step. "The more we make of ourselves, the less we actually exist." Real self-fulfillment occurs, and I would hazard to say we only find our real self, when we realize—become aware of and make real—the fact that we are part of something bigger than us. Call it compassion, call it dependent co-arising (as Buddhists teach), call it what you will. Merton wrote that our own inner ground is where we are "mysteriously present at once to myself *and* to the freedoms of all [others]." We give that fulfilled self away.

The Scripture scholar N. T. Wright describes the *telos*, the ultimate end of Christian life, as, according to Scripture, *a new heaven and a new earth.*[4] One day I need to realize that it's not all about me! This whole enterprise of human life is not just about me dying and escaping my body and going to heaven. It's about a new heaven and a new earth. And I am a part of a whole trajectory of all creation that is *groaning and in labor pains.*[5] Sometimes even what we think of as our true self has to die to take its place as a part of the greater whole. Dogen, the father of the Soto school of Japanese Buddhism, says famously, that *to forget the self is to be actualized by myriad things.* There's a marvelous allusion in the Gospel of John when Jesus says that the Father *'not only prunes away every barren branch, but he trims clean the fruitful ones to increase their yield.'*[6] In other words, sometimes the good branches get trimmed too. What we are always looking for is not just the good, but the greatest good, the *summum bonum.* Another agricultural image from the Gospel of John: *'Unless a grain of wheat falls into the ground and dies it remains a single grain, but if it dies it shall yield a rich harvest.'*[7] Pope Benedict wrote that this phrase sums up the meaning of all of Jesus' parables.

There's one further element to this. When John points out the Lamb of God to two of his own disciples, in a sense he is sending them away to follow Jesus instead of keeping them to himself. One of them turns out to be the future apostle Andrew who immediately goes off and gets his brother Simon,

---

[4] This image appears three times in the Bible: Is 65:17; 2 Pt 3:13; Rev 21:21.
[5] Rom 8:22.
[6] Jn 15:2.
[7] Jn 12:24.

whom Jesus will name Peter. So John has prepared the way, trained these two disciples, and he points out to them the Lamb of God, the one who ranks ahead of him—and then he decreases so that Christ may increase. And Andrew himself is called the *protoclete* in Greek, the "first called," because he is indeed the first one called by Jesus. But even though he was the first called, before he stays with Jesus he goes to get his brother Simon, and then immediately takes a back seat to him. This too is our role as community, the summons for the greater good, not the summons only for ourselves.

And so the challenge, the summons to us as individuals and as a community, is multilayered. First of all, to listen to the still small voice calling us in our own hearts: What do you want? Remember: Sometimes that voice, like God's call to Samuel, is only heard in the silence and the holy darkness of night—and what silence of mind and heart we need to hear it! And then we need instruction, we need to lean back on our teachers, friends, and mentors to understand and interpret that call. One step further is to listen to the summons of the specific place we have been planted with its specific problems and needs, and to figure out how we are part of its evolution and growth. And finally, to be like Eli, John the Baptist, and Andrew for others, to call forth gifts from those around us, not to be threatened by someone else shining and thriving, but to encourage those gifts and those people for the sake of their own perfecting and for the sake of the greater good.

Ultimately for us all to say, with every breath, the only prayer really worth saying: *Here I am. I come to do your will.* Like Jesus' own mantra, embedded right in the middle of the Lord's Prayer and even in the garden of his agony: Thy will be done. Thy will be done. Thy will be done.

7

Prisoners of Hope

On the Energy of Love

I have got quite a propensity for citing a plethora of sources and quoting all kinds of people who are smarter and more enlightened than I am to back up my own intuitions and arguments. And for the topic of hope I feel as if I could simply string together pearls of other people's wisdom. And the first person I want to quote is a brilliant Jesuit priest: While we were walking the streets of Milwaukee together near Lake Michigan many years ago, he said something that I have consequently thought of and repeated countless times: "Hope is a seed that never dies."

Real hope, you see, is one of what we call the theological virtues that we believe are *infused* in us by God. The Catechism of the Catholic Church (#1813) says that hope "responds to the aspiration to happiness which God has placed in every human heart." (That ought to sound familiar to an American. The Preamble to our Constitution declares that we are "endowed by our creator with certain inalienable rights, and among these are life, liberty, and the pursuit of happiness.") God has placed the aspiration to happiness in every human heart. And because it is divinely infused, it never really dies.

I would add the caveat, though, that there are persons, places, and things that can block or stunt the growth of that seed, like the sprout from that seed becoming trapped under a large boulder. Perhaps a good part of our ministry of healing involves removing such boulders from human hearts and minds as well as from and in concrete conditions.

Before we go any further though, we need to clarify what the virtue of hope is *not*. First of all, the *virtue* of hope is not *wishful thinking*. That's of course how we usually use the word: "I hope we are going to have pizza for dinner. I hope my grandmother recovers from her illness. I hope it won't rain." We will probably continue to use the word in that way, but in some way I want to ruin it for you. Hope isn't just a wish: It's a surety. It's something we believe. Our theological hope is just that, rooted in a belief.

I don't want to get into the weeds of Scholastic definitions here, but of course it goes without saying that hope goes along with the two other theological virtues—faith and love. The classic formulation comes from Saint Augustine: "There's no love without hope. There's no hope without love. And there's neither hope nor love without faith."

We could think of these three theological virtues—faith, hope, and love—as really three aspects of one thing. Clement of Alexandria in the second century referred to these three as the *hagia trias*, "the holy triad." Or maybe better, we could think of this holy triad as a "perichoresis" of sorts, as we say about the relationship among the Persons of the Trinity: There is never one without the other, receiving from and giving way to the other. No love without hope, no hope without love, and neither hope nor love without faith.

I don't mean this as any kind of definitive theological statement, but I've come to think of this holy triad in this way: Faith is the content, hope is the energy, and love is the action.

We usually confuse faith and hope. As we have established, hope isn't wishful thinking. It's sure knowledge, sure knowledge of and commitment to that content, and that content is faith. We even speak in our old-fashioned language about "the deposit of faith." Let's say faith is the content, the deposit, and hope then becomes the energy. I recognize that all three have a level of feeling to them as well—faith as trust, hope as confidence, love as sentiment. However, we can't always count on the feeling. Jesus cannot and does not command us to feel something for someone, but he does command us to love as he loved, washing feet, welcoming the stranger.

But—and this is a piece of wisdom I overheard on the radio one day—"Hope isn't wishful thinking; it's full of requirements." Hope demands of us to do something. That's why I say it's the energy. And that's what love is, what hope requires us to do. So, if faith is the content and hope is the energy, love is the action. Love is faith-and-hope incarnated, embodied. In other words, love isn't necessarily just a feeling; it's a way of being and, even more, it's an action. It's not a passive thing. Jesus doesn't command us to feel anything, but he does command us to do something: *'Love one another as I have loved you. Love your neighbor as yourself. Love your enemies!'*[1] And the energy of that love is hope, hope that the actions of love will ultimately conquer.

Here let me bring in another great voice on another thing hope is not. Vaclav Havel was the Czech poet, author, playwright, and political dissident who became a great statesman. He was the last president of Czechoslovakia until its dissolution, and the first president of the Czech Republic from 1993

---

[1] Jn 13:35; Mk 12:30 (Lev 19:18); Mt 5:44.

until 2003. According to Havel, "Hope is a state of mind." Hope "is a dimension of the soul . . . an orientation of the spirit." However, he says, "It is not the same thing as joy that things are going well," at least not in the short term, "but rather an ability to work for something because it is good, not just because it stands a chance to succeed. . . . Hope is not the conviction that something will turn out well, but the certainty that something makes sense, regardless how it turns out."

So, you see, that's not wishful thinking, and that's why I call its action "love." Love is doing something simply because it is good, because it's the right thing to do, not just because it stands a chance to succeed. Of course, the prime example is the crucified Jesus; his hope was in something far greater and more mysterious than worldly success. Love is not a feeling; it's an action, a conviction. We talk about "tough love." Well, in this way of thinking, *all* of love is tough. That's the movement from thinking like a child to thinking like an adult that Paul sings about in his great hymn to love in the Letter to the Corinthians.

Here's the next thing that hope is not: Hope is also not the same as *optimism*. And here I want to bring in my favorite quote of all time on this topic, from the philosopher and activist Cornel West. He says, "The categories of optimism and pessimism don't exist for me." Why? Because "I'm a blues man," he says. "A blues man is a prisoner of hope, and hope is a qualitatively different category than optimism. Optimism is a secular construct, a calculation of probability," as Havel said. "But we are people of hope," Professor West says. "Hope wrestles with despair, but it doesn't generate optimism. It just generates this energy to be courageous, to bear witness"—there it is, hope generates *energy*!—"to see what the end is going to be. No guarantee, unfinished, open-ended. I am a prisoner of hope. I'm going to die full of hope," he says. "There's no doubt about that because that is a choice I make."

And then he ends by saying, "But at the same time, the end doesn't look too good right now."

I love that phrase—prisoner of hope. But I tend to turn that last bit around: "The end doesn't look too good right now, but I'm a prisoner of hope." A friend who was very close to the late Jesuit peace activist and poet Daniel Berrigan said that he thought Professor West had gotten that phrase from Berrigan. But it actually has its roots in the prophets, which would be no surprise for either Berrigan or West. Specifically it comes from Zechariah 9:12: *Return to your stronghold, O prisoners of hope; today I declare that I will restore to you double.*

And here I want to bring in one other powerful voice, this one from Thomas Merton, again on what hope is not. It's not wishful thinking. It is not a sunny, naïve, and, as I heard someone else say, "hysterical optimism." That kind of optimism can actually numb us, like a palliative. And that's the third thing hope is not: a *palliative*. Remember what a palliative is: In medicine it's something that relieves symptoms without dealing with the causes of the condition. It's what we give to someone who is going to die when we've given up all hope. The blistering line from Merton is when he writes about how authentic hope is "married to a firm refusal to accept any palliatives or anything that cheats hope by pretending to relieve apparent despair." I think too often religion in general (and especially religious music) can function as a kind of sugarcoated palliative, the nature of which is only to take away the pain with sunny optimism, not to cure the disease. Like so many of the inane platitudes we say to people when they are grieving, when sometimes it's better to cry with them or just sit with them.

Hope is not a palliative; it takes despair seriously and

wrestles with it, while all the while it never stops believing in an ultimate positive end.

The Letter to the Hebrews says that *hope is placed before us like a firm and sure anchor, it extends beyond the veil through which Jesus has entered on our behalf.*[2] This is a strong image, being firmly rooted, grounded, "like a sure anchor," as well as extending into the heavenly realm, "beyond the veil." Or we might say, with Jesus, *'on earth as it is in heaven.'* We may need to clarify our belief about the reign of God while we're at it. It is not ultimately two separate realms, one on earth and one in "some heaven light years away." According to the Gospels there is only one reign of God that Jesus preaches about—and it's *'on earth as it is in heaven.'* It's both a firm anchor, rooted in the earth, and it extends beyond the heavenly veil where Jesus has gone, "stretching out his hands between heaven and earth," as the Eucharistic Prayer reads, taking his body and the rest of creation with him. And so that central line of the Lord's Prayer: *'Thy will be done on earth as it is in heaven.'* There's only one reign of God.

Incidentally, of the three theological virtues it is hope that takes the form of prayer, and specifically the Lord's Prayer is a great example of that. We hope for absolute redemption when we pray *'Thy kingdom come'*; and we also hope for the necessities of life here and now when we ask God to *'give us this day our daily bread'* because, as Saint Augustine taught, these two requests, for daily bread and the coming of the reign of God, are indivisibly bound together. And it's that indivisibility of worldly needs and the world's redemption that makes hope one of the most important impulses for Christian involvement in the political realm at all, especially

---

[2] Heb 6:19–20.

on issues of social justice and civil rights. Hope "responds to the aspiration to happiness which God has placed in every human heart." We have been endowed by our Creator with the inalienable rights to life, liberty, and the pursuit of happiness, on earth as it is in heaven.

And probably the best articulation of this is the line famously spoken by and associated with Rev. Dr. Martin Luther King Jr.: "The arc of the moral universe is long, but it bends toward justice." The original version of this saying is attributed to a nineteenth-century Unitarian minister named Theodore Parker, a prominent American Transcendentalist who was a forceful advocate for the abolition of slavery. The allusion to the arc of the moral universe comes from a sermon titled "Of Justice and the Conscience" published in 1853. Why would someone keep on fighting even if the end doesn't look too good right now? Why would someone do what is right even if it doesn't look like it has a chance to succeed? Reverend Parker explained:

> We cannot understand the moral Universe. The arc is a long one, and our eyes reach but a little way; we cannot calculate the curve and complete the figure by the experience of sight; but we can divine it by conscience, and we surely know that it bends toward justice. Justice will not fail, though wickedness appears strong, and has on its side the armies and thrones of power, the riches and the glory of the world. And though [the poor] crouch down in despair, justice will not fail and perish out from the world . . . nor will what is really wrong and contrary to God's law of justice continually endure.

There's a line from the Letter to the Corinthians that is apropos here, with practical as well as mystical implications:

that *God may be all in all*.[3] Our hope is based on the belief that at the culmination of the entire arc of history God will be all in all. There's a phrase that often gets attributed to John Lennon of the Beatles and sometimes to Oscar Wilde, both of whom might have expressed this sentiment in some form, but whose origin seems to be with the Brazilian writer Fernando Sabino, speaking of his father. Sabino wrote, "Perhaps the best thing that I can remember is what he said to me one day when he found me in the grip of a mental affliction: 'My son, everything works out in the end. If it hasn't, it's because it hasn't come to an end yet.' "

This is the faith that gives me the energy (hope) to do the action of love: God will be all in all. "Everything works out in the end. If it hasn't, it's because it hasn't come to an end yet," because "the arc of the moral universe is long, but it bends toward justice." There's our hope. The sure anchor, believing that God will be all in all, on earth as it is in heaven.

∽

There are two times in my life when I was actually speechless, literally *could not speak*, could not get words out of my mouth. The first was President Obama's inauguration in 2009. I promise you, I do not want to get partisan here, but Republican or Democrat, one has to recognize that this was an astounding thing, that a Black man had been elected and was about to assume the Presidency of the United States when, for example, just forty-four years earlier 600 unarmed peaceful civil rights protesters were attacked on the Edmund Pettus Bridge with billy clubs and sprayed with tear gas, while marching for voting rights for Black people. And at least one of those protesters was sitting in the crowd that day, beam-

---

[3] 1 Cor 15:28.

ing with pride, eyes brimming with tears—Representative John Lewis.

But it wasn't President Obama that got to me. It was Aretha Franklin singing "My Country 'Tis of Thee." Aretha, the Queen of Soul, singing that song, there on the Capitol Steps. I happened to be with two friends from England that morning and as 'Retha was singing, I turned to them wanting to explain the significance of it and I opened my mouth . . . and nothing came out. Aretha. Singing that song. There. For that event. And I thought, "There's hope."

The letter to the Hebrews goes on to say, *God is not unjust; God will not forget your work.* "Hope is not wishful thinking; it's full of requirements." Our hope is rooted in how we live our lives, in what we do each moment of each day; our hope is anchored where we invest our energy and what we have to do to uncover whatever is stunting the growth of that seed that is planted in us, nurturing it to grow and bear fruit. It's not a dull lifeless thing: Hope is a "fervor that I feel like a fire in my bones," as one of my favorite songwriters wrote. Hope is not wishful thinking; it's full of requirements! Just like our beloved democracy: it's full of requirements to keep it alive. It takes tough love.

However, one of the consequences of our actions of love inspired by hope is that exercising it may also lead to the cross. Like President Lincoln, like Dr. King, like Oscar Romero, like Ita Ford, Maura Clarke, Dorothy Kazel, and Jean Donovan, the women missionaries who were beaten, raped, and murdered in El Salvador in 1980. Like countless martyrs persecuted for the sake of righteousness. But again, *God is not unjust; God will not forget our work.* There's a promise that awaits the faithful, the hopeful, the loving. And that promise, of course, is the sure anchor of our hope. As the Scriptures promise us three times: *We await a new heaven and a new earth.* And God will be all in all. Again, the prime example is the Risen Christ, whose hope was anchored in something far greater and more mysterious than worldly success.

☙

One last step: I'm not sure it happens to everybody, but I think we all are supposed to reach a time in our lives when we realize that the work we are doing is not for ourselves, that "my life is not about me." Parents tend to get that; sometimes celibate male religious like me don't. But it became clear to me when I took over as superior of my monastic community. I realized early on that I was not supposed to be building the community that I wanted; I was supposed to be shoring up the community that I thought monks were going to need in the years ahead.

When I was serving as prior, I had a quote from John Cardinal Dearden tacked to the bulletin board in my office for a long time. He served as archbishop of Detroit from 1959 to 1980 and was one of the American pillars of the Second Vatican Council for which he served on the doctrinal commission. This was part of a speech he first presented in 1979. (Pope Francis also quoted it in 2015 in his remarks to the Roman Curia.) Every now and then, he said, it helps to step back and take a long view. That's when we realize that the Reign of God is not only beyond our efforts; it is even beyond our *vision*. What we accomplish in our lifetime is only a tiny fraction of the magnificent enterprise that is God's work. Nothing we do is complete, no statement, no prayer, no confession, no pastoral program accomplishes everything.

So he says, "This is what we are about." And here to me is hope: We plant the seeds that one day will grow. We water seeds already planted, knowing that they hold future promise. We lay foundations that will need further development. We provide yeast that produces far beyond our capabilities. We cannot do everything, and there is *actually* a sense of liberation in realizing that. This enables us to do something, and to do it very well. It may be incomplete, but it is a beginning, a step along the way, an opportunity for the Lord's grace to enter and do the rest.

And here's the closing line that I had tacked to my bulletin board: "We are prophets of a future not our own."

∽

Let me tell you about the other time I was struck mute, when my niece Elyse was born. My younger sister asked me to be in the operating room when her second child was born, by C-section, which was one of the greatest honors of my life. At one point during the procedure the doctor said, "Does anyone want to see the baby?" And so I peeked over the operating screen, and he just had her little head out of the incision. I gasped and then I turned to Dina, my sister, and I tried to speak, and nothing would come out of my mouth. To see that miracle, to be a witness of that event, was simply overwhelming. One moment she was not there, she was in my sister's belly. And the next moment she was there, gasping for air and crying.

One of the things that keeps striking me as I get older is that people are still having babies, still starting families. I must say, some days I feel downright apocalyptic, between the economic inequality, wars, global warming, the rise of nationalism and xenophobia, and the lunatics and tyrants who are in charge of large countries. And yet here are these people going along as if life is going to continue. Producing another generation of human beings, hoping that they will get it better than we did. This is a sure sign of hope as that seed that never dies.

I had held on to an article written by one of my favorite writers, Adam Gopnik, for decades, about the birth of his daughter that had moved me in a way I didn't even understand until I witnessed Elyse's birth. Gopnik wrote that as he watched the sleeping mom and the tiny newborn in her arms, he had a moment of revelation, a religious vision. And he realized that having a baby isn't about starting over, a clean slate with endless possibility, or a new beginning. "A birth is not a rebirth," he says. It's a weighty event precisely because in a telescopic universe for one moment we see microscopically. There's a singularity in the whole cosmos as another child comes into the world. The world may seem like a meaningless place, and we may be just "weird, replicating mammals on its surface." And yet

> the whole purpose of the universe since it began was, in a way, to produce this baby, who is the tiny end point of a funnel that goes back to the beginning of time—a singularity that history was pointing toward from the start. . . . The universe doesn't need a purpose, if life goes on. You sink back and hear the nurse cooing . . . to the mother and child . . . and feel as completely useless as any other male animal after a birth and, at the same time, somehow serenely powerful, beyond care or criticism, since you have taken part in the only really majestic choice we get to make in life, which is to continue it.[4]

---

[4] Adam Gopnik, *New Yorker*, January 31, 2000.

That's hope. And I am a prisoner of hope. I'm going to die full of hope. It's not just wishful thinking or a calculation of the probability of success. It's not naïve optimism or a palliative that takes away the pain without offering a cure. It's a seed that never dies, that generates energy to be courageous and bear witness, a dimension of the soul, an orientation of the spirit. And it's a choice I make, a majestic choice—to continue life, a prophet of a future not my own, believing that all will be right in the end. Because, though the world may seem like a meaningless place at times, that's only because its moral arc is long, beyond the range of our vision and the capacity of our best efforts.

But God has revealed to the wise ones who have gone before us, and thus they have told us, that the arc of history bends toward God's justice, and in the end God will be all in all, on earth as it is in heaven.

8

A Time for Everything

On Prophecy

I remember the first time I really dove deeply into Qoheleth, the Book of Ecclesiastes, and how awed I was by the opening lines. There's nothing else like it in the Bible.

> Vanity of vanities, says the Teacher. . . . All is
>   vanity.
> What do people gain from all the toil at which
>   they toil under the sun?
> A generation goes, and a generation comes,
>   but the earth remains for ever.
> . . . All streams run to the sea, but the sea is
>   not full;
> to the place where the streams flow, there they
>   continue to flow.
> All things are wearisome; more than one can
>   express.[1]

---

[1] Eccl 1:2–4, 7–8.

It's like a world-weary soliloquy. There's a sad sweetness about it that sets the tone for the entire book. I was studying a lot about Buddhism at that time, and I was seeing the futility that "the Teacher" speaks about in a new way, in the light of the dependent co-arising that the Buddha taught was the underlying reality to existence, and the absence of any permanent self of anything, the realization of which leads to enlightenment. The futility of seeking Wisdom, the futility of self-indulgence—everything is vanity.

And yet, despite this futility, perhaps the best-known verse of the book, from Chapter 3—*For everything there is a season, and a time for every matter under heaven: a time to be born, a time to die*[2]—strikes me as having a certain strength and serenity about it, an acceptance of things as they are, even a kind of abandonment to divine providence.

Some will remember that that particular passage was made popular in a song called "Turn Turn Turn," written by the famous songwriter Pete Seeger many years ago. Seeger was the leader of the folk music scene that was sweeping America in the late 1950s. He and his group, the Weavers, had had a major hit with the song "Goodnight, Irene." But the folk movement had started shifting pretty deeply into protest songs by this time, the early years of the so-called Cold War. This was a precursor to an even deeper move in that direction the next decade with songs promoting civil rights and others protesting the war in Vietnam. Seeger's publisher was urging him to write another hit song and asked him, "Why can't you write another song like 'Goodnight, Irene'? I can't sell or promote these protest songs." (Of course, the irony is that Pete Seeger hadn't written "Goodnight, Irene" either. It was written by the folk and blues singer Lead Belly.) Seeger

---

[2] Eccl 3:1–8.

wrote back saying, "You better find another songwriter. This is the only kind of song I know how to write."

But one day he was flipping through a little pocket notebook that he kept to jot down ideas for songs, and he found some passages from the Bible that he had copied into it, especially, as he said later, some "verses by a bearded fellow with sandals, a tough-minded fellow called Ecclesiastes." He wound up using that passage from Chapter 3 almost verbatim; he just added the refrain, "To everything turn, turn, turn, / there is a season turn, turn, turn . . ." and then tagged on his own hopeful concluding line for the Cold War audience: "a time for peace—I swear it's not too late." (That's why the later recording by the group the Byrds, arguably the most famous version of the song, became an anthem for the Vietnam War era as well.) Now for Pete Seeger, it actually was another protest song. But his publisher—another irony— didn't seem to get it, and he wrote back saying, "Wonderful! Just what I'd hoped for."

Like his friend Woody Guthrie, Seeger was a seminal figure in an era when popular music was beginning its slow evolution away from soothing whimsical feel-good pieces to being a prophetic voice in culture. I love what the great man had etched on the face of his banjo: "This machine surrounds hate and forces it to surrender."

∽

One of the strongest images I have from my brief but intense pilgrimage to the Holy Land is of Rabbi Eli, who was probably the closest thing to one of the Hebrew prophets I have ever met. This was an Israeli who had been arrested several times for standing in solidarity with Palestinians, protesting the human rights violations against them, and trying to protect their land against the far-right faction of Zionists. We were standing at a high spot in East Jerusalem looking out over the disputed territories, and Rabbi Eli was pointing out the various iterations of the security wall making its serpentine way through Palestinian land. He was showing us a map of a new settlement about to begin construction in defiance of the UN and the US, which would effectively cut Palestine in half, thus preventing any possibility of Palestinians ever having a contiguous piece of land to call their state and effectively destroying the so-called two-state solution. Rabbi Eli said, "And so we are asking ourselves: What time is it? Is it a quarter to midnight? Is it five minutes to midnight? With this development I think it's one minute to midnight. It's almost too late."

That moment seared so deeply in my mind that on the way home on the plane I wrote a whole song about it called "One Minute to Midnight," the closest thing to a '60s-style protest song I had ever written. One of the verses included lines that were my sadly ironic version of the famous verses from the prophet Isaiah: "We've beaten our ploughshares back into swords / and made spears of our pruning hooks." And I added, "We've turned revelation to a battle of words / and made weapons of our holy books."

I wrote another song during that era that I've never sung in public, but I sing to myself all the time.

> Everybody's goin' the wrong way, the wrong
>   way.
> Everybody's goin' the wrong way.
> You and me are goin' the wrong way, the
>   wrong way.
> You and me are goin' the wrong way.

Not ev'ry road is gonna lead up the mountain.
Some of them keep goin' around and 'round.
Every now and then you gotta stop what
    you're doin',
gotta change what you're thinking and
turn around, turn around . . .

Everybody's goin' the wrong way, the wrong
    way.
Everybody's goin' the wrong way . . .

We have two liturgical periods of preparation in the Christian tradition, four weeks before Christmas and forty days before Easter. They both used to be thought of as penitential seasons (the priest even wore the same color vestments for both seasons, violet). St. Benedict in his Rule for Monks says that a monk's whole life should be a little Lent. With all due respect, I think of my whole life like a little Advent. It's different from Lent in subtle ways. It has a strange sense of time, and it's filled with a kind of joyful expectation. I don't think of Advent so much as a penitential season, but as a *prophetic* one, and that's another reason I like it so much. So yes, we're cleaning house: "make your house fair as you are able," the hymn says, because "Love, the guest, is on the way," which may sound whimsical and joyous, dancing around the living room with a dust mop and music playing in the background and the smell of a pudding baking in the oven. But that housecleaning is not a light thing. While everyone else is doing their Christmas shopping, we first spend a few weeks listening to the prophets in our liturgical texts, particularly the prophet Isaiah. We get challenged at the micro level and the macro at the same time, from our individual lives to the big picture and everything in between. We get challenged to ask ourselves individually, "What time is it in my life?"

in the same way we are supposed to be asking ourselves as a church, as a species, as a world, "What time is it? Where are we headed?" They're all related, those questions, inextricably linked together.

At a micro level we might be asking, "How long can I continue to abuse my body before it's too late and I descend into some kind of debilitating health condition?" My Dad never quit smoking until he had his quadruple bypass; my uncle never quit drinking until he died of sclerosis of the liver. "When am I going to heal that relationship with my parents, my old friend, my co-worker? When am I going to do my own inner work before I have let my dysfunctional relationships tear my family or my community or my workplace apart? Maybe I'll do it later, after I catch up on social media."

Wake up! Do you know what time it is?

That's what the prophets ask, like Pete Seeger, like Rabbi Eli. "Do you know what time it is?" Prophets don't predict the future; they predict the present. Prophets tell us what time it is, in our personal lives as well as in our communal lives, and they say, "If you keep on this course, this is what is going to happen."

☙

I want to add one more "a time for" to Qoheleth's list: There's "a time for acceptance and a time for agency." As I get older, the more I am attentive to the proper proportion of these two things, when to step in with a directive word or corrective action and when to simply let things take their course. Or, as Jesus teaches, when to uproot the weeds growing up among the wheat and when to allow them to grow and toss them in the fire later.[3] I've learned some of this from the prophetic

---

[3] Mt 13:24–30.

voices in my own life, or, at times, the lack of them. There are times when someone has stopped me with a word or an action, loved me enough to tell me that I was on absolutely the wrong path. Those were prophetic voices in my life. There are other times when I wish someone had cared enough to step in. There's a time for everything, and sometimes we can miss the moment.

I tend to think of this acceptance-agency balance in my own life as the Asian contemplative aspect in tension with the Western active energy, like the yin-yang of Taoism, both of which I find present and active in me in equal parts. If there is a danger to the contemplative side, it is in a kind of quietism, a sin of omission, if you will, even at times a lethargic lack of energy or a reluctance to break out of my contemplative comfort. If there is a cautionary note concerning the active side, it is in its surety, as well as its compulsivity, and the danger of universalizing and then imposing one's own views and solutions, however accurate and well-discerned they may or may not be. My intuition is that there can come a time in our lives, a moment of great maturity, when, as the Twelve Step program promises, we "intuitively know how to handle situations which used to baffle us," when to sit back and when to act, when to be silent and when to speak. The Tao te Ching and the Bhagavad Gita at their best lead us to this kind of wisdom as well, when it is as if the doer disappears into what we theists might call the will of God. *It is no longer I who live, but it is Christ who lives in me.*[4]

This tension too can play out from the micro to the macro, from the individual to the communal and corporate. At what point do I accept the limitations of my physical capabilities and the inevitable process of aging, and when does that

---

[4] Gal 2:20.

become sheer laziness or simple fatigue on my part? When do I try to address dysfunction in my family or community system and how much time and energy do I invest before I simply "stick to my side of the street"? When is the right moment for me to join my voice or even add my physical presence to a social protest or an act of civil disobedience calling out a social evil?

I know in my own life I have often had a tendency to think that when I get it all together, then I am going to take care of this, or that, or the other thing. This is often an avoidance of our own mortality and a denial of the fragility of human existence. *The day of the Lord may come* for us *like a thief in the night,* Scripture tells us.[5] Maybe we think, "After I'm fully enlightened, then I'll start to give my life in service; then I'll worry about other people; then I'll start to pay attention to what's going on around me." It doesn't work that way. The same applies to charity, at every level from the individual through the communal and the corporate: We're not supposed to wait until we're financially comfortable to take care of the poor in our midst. Just as there is no way to peace—peace itself is the way, so we don't wait to be compassionate until we're enlightened: Compassion is part of the way to enlightenment.

In his book *In the Absence of God,* Sam Keen had a pretty strong critique of contemporary spirituality. For years he was a big supporter of all kinds of experiments with alternate, especially non-Western, forms of spirituality, but he wrote that he eventually grew dissatisfied, partially because the whole movement "has largely been irrelevant to the great social, political and economic problems we face." It doesn't do soup kitchens, civil rights' marches or protests. "Amid all

---

[5] Mt 24:43; 1 Thes 5:2; Rev 16:15.

the offerings on holistic healing, awareness, opening the heart, oneness, knowing God, and sacred bodywork, there is little or no reference to justice." So it's no surprise, he says, that the new spiritual movements haven't produced a Dietrich Bonhoeffer or a Reinhold Niebuhr, a Gandhi, a Dorothy Day, a Martin Luther King Jr., or a Cesar Chavez.

In other words, it is not prophetic.

Do we really even want to know what time it is?

❧

So, let's talk about the macro.

For several reasons, along with the phrase "East-West" I have stopped using the term "Judeo-Christian." Instead, I use a phrase that is sometimes employed in the field of comparative religion and refer to the "prophetic traditions." One reason for this is because "the prophetic traditions" includes all three Abrahamic faiths, Islam as well as Judaism and Christianity, and I feel we need to do everything we can to be in solidarity wherever and however we can with the good people of Islam, with whom we have much in common. One commonality, for instance, besides our common ancestor, is that we are all three *revealed* religions, believing as we do that the Scriptures are God's purposeful self-manifestation. (The Qur'an respects this common ground and refers to our three religions as *Ahl al-kitab*, "People of the Book.")

Right along with that, our three traditions share an understanding of time. Whereas the Asian traditions tend to view time as cyclical, even something to be escaped, the prophetic traditions see time as a *sacrament*, something God uses for our sanctification. History is salvation history. It's going somewhere—to the reign of God. We have a cyclical sense of time as well, following the seasons of each year, which is especially important in our ritual and sacramental life. In our remembrance of something each day, each week, each year, such as the Exodus or the Last Supper, we believe that the power of the original event is just as strong, just as real, just as present as it was in the original event, in the eternal present of God. But even that cycle of the seasons is a kind of tightening funnel heading toward what Teilhard called an Omega Point, a fullness of time when, as Paul says, *God will be all in all.*[6] We're going somewhere. And it's from that sense of time that we derive our sense of hope. And our sense of prophecy, "reading the signs of the times with the eyes of faith." For everything there is a season. Everything is going to be all right in the end—*God will be all in all.*

There are times when it's okay to sit back and let things take their course. And then there are times when you want to scream because it seems so obvious, beyond a shadow of a doubt, that something is simply not going the right way, like a train hurling itself off a cliff.

My friends told me that when I came back from that trip to the Holy Land my preaching changed. It was more fiery, more "prophetic," I suppose. I was fired up by the frustration and energized by the agitation that I felt witnessing up close a situation that was patently unsustainable and obviously unjust, but with no visible solution and no one with enough real moral authority to "fix" everything. And I think I felt like never before the challenge of being a follower of Jesus, and I glimpsed what a privileged position we Christians have there in the Holy Land as well as in the world at large, to stand in the breach between our Jewish and Muslim brothers and sisters and dare to preach love of our enemies, dare to

---

[6] 1 Cor 15:28.

believe that peace is possible, dare to take Jesus at his word.

"Everbody's goin' the wrong way, the wrong way. Everybody's goin' the wrong way . . ."

I remember a few years back when a huge storm ripped through the US over the Thanksgiving holiday. The meteorologists named it "Boreas" after the Greek god of the north wind. While we were eating our lunch on Thanksgiving Day, 14 people were killed, and another 58 million people were stranded or had lost power. Climate scientists predict that extreme weather events of all types are going to increase in their frequency and their severity, and there is overwhelming agreement in the scientific community that our carbon fuel–based way of life is a huge contributing factor. And yet the United Nations summit on climate change in Warsaw that very same month was considered to be the most ineffectual *ever*. We, as a human race, are still not willing to have the conversation about how our lifestyles may have to change, from our approach to transportation and architecture to our consumer habits. Do we know what time it is? Do we care? In this case it may actually be a few seconds to midnight, not only too late to turn it around, but also too late to stop it.

There's a time for acceptance, for Qoheleth's patience. And then there are times for real prophetic voices. "Everybody's goin' the wrong way, the wrong way . . ."

Another of the times to make our voices heard is when injustice is being done to the weak, as we learn from the prophets. This is also echoed in the psalms and then reinvigorated in the Beatitudes, where we hear over and over that God's power is always and only a power exercised on behalf of those who need it—the poor, the outcast, the despised, the marginalized, the wretched and lonely, the abandoned. Take Psalm 37, for instance: *Yet a little while, and the wicked will be no more; though you look diligently for their place, they will not be there. But the meek shall inherit the land and delight themselves in abundant prosperity.*[7] And not only the meek; according to Jesus also those who mourn, those who hunger and thirst for righteousness, the merciful, those who suffer for justice, and the peacemakers.

Even popes get criticized when they become what is considered too social (read "prophetic") in their message. (There was the famous "Mater, si, Magister, no" headline of the American magazine *National Review* in 1961 in a negative response to Pope John XXIII's social encyclical *Mater et Magister*, though it must be admitted that that phrase has been applied to both conservatives and liberals who pick and choose what aspects of the Church's teaching they will support.) Even a stalwart of old-world values such as Benedict XVI addressed contemporary Catholic sociology as much as if not more than doctrine or discipline and tried over and over again to mend the seeming split between the Church's pro-life and peace-and-justice wings. In *Caritas in Veritate*, for instance, he insisted on the link between what he called "human ecology," meaning the Church's teaching on pro-life issues, and "natural ecology," including the environment as well as the economy, arguing that defending the unborn child and defending the poor are two sides of the same coin. Just as Pope Paul VI was famous for the line, "If you want peace work for justice," Benedict's 2010 message for World Peace Day was titled "If You Want Peace, Protect the Environment." This is similar to how Pope Francis addressed the division between those Catholics who are invested in what Pope John Paul II called the "new evangelization" as opposed to those who are more interested in the "social Gospel," the poor, immigrants, and the environment, our opposition to war, the arms trade, the death penalty and

---

[7] Ps 37:10.

so on. As if they were two different things! He did the same thing in the apostolic exhortation "The Joy of the Gospel." He wrote that there is a "social dimension of evangelization" that we are not free to ignore. And if "this dimension is not properly brought out," he writes, "there is a constant risk of distorting the authentic and integral meaning of the mission of evangelization" because "both Christian preaching and life are meant to have an impact on society."

In other words, we stop being a prophetic voice if we don't apply the gospel to the real situation in the real world.

∽

The Lutheran pastor Munther Isaac, who I think is a truly prophetic voice in our day and age, wrote that the irony for Palestinian Christians is that some Evangelical Christians (and he may be addressing particularly American Evangelicals), with what he thinks is their overemphasis on prophecy, have actually lost the capacity for being prophetic. Many American Evangelicals, for example, tend to see modern Israel through the lens of biblical prophecy that foretells the revival of a Jewish homeland. This is appealing to the so-called Christian right because many of them believe that a mass return of Jewish people to the Holy Land will bring about the Second Coming of Christ. They would be totally against the two-state solution, therefore, because, as one prominent pastor stated, for them there is no such thing as Palestine, the West Bank or an occupation, since Abraham and his heirs were given title to the land by God.[8] ("We've

---

[8] My own communion, the Catholic Church advocates for a two-state solution, as does the United States Conference of Catholic Bishops, with both Israel and Palestine coexisting peacefully. In 2015, the Vatican of-

turned revelation to a battle of words / and made weapons of our holy books.")

Pastor Isaac, a Palestinian Christian and a Scripture scholar, begs to differ. If you want to prove the Bible is right, he says, you don't do it by pointing to world events as prophecy fulfillment. "We prove that the Bible is right by radical obedience to the teachings of Jesus—by proving that Jesus' teachings actually work and that they can make the world a better place."

What does that look like? It means loving our enemies, turning the other cheek. It means praying (sometimes out loud) for those who persecute us and forgiving those who sin against us. Feeding the poor, caring for the oppressed, walking the extra mile. Being inclusive and not exclusive. "And maybe, only maybe then," Pastor Isaac says, "the world will start to take us seriously and believe in our Bible." Not only that, Jesus adds a warning too. After the Beatitudes and all the other words of consolation addressed to the anawim in the Sermon on the Mount, the poor ones so beloved by God in the Hebrew Scriptures, Jesus ends by saying

> "Not everyone who says to me, 'Lord, Lord,' will enter the kingdom of heaven, but only the one who does the will of my Father in heaven. On that day many will say to me, 'Lord, Lord, did we not prophesy in your name...?' Then I will declare to them, 'I never knew you; go away from me, you evildoers.'"[9]

And then he adds, '*everyone who hears these words of mine*'—and the words he is referring to, by the way, are the

---

ficially recognized the State of Palestine, a move intended to promote negotiations and peaceful resolution.

[9] Mt 7:21–23.

Beatitudes and the Sermon on the Mount that he has just preached, which tell us who and how we are to be in the world—'*everyone who hears these words of mine and does not act on them will be like a foolish man who built his house on sand. The rain fell, and the floods came, and the winds blew and beat against that house, and it fell—and great was its fall!*'[10] There's a sound prophecy, from Jesus' own lips. The way you are living, moving, and being in the world is leading you nowhere! It's a house built on sand. My way, the way of the Gospel, Jesus tells his listeners and tells us, the way of the peacemakers and the poor, the way of footwashers, the way of crucified love is ultimately the right way to God's will being done—both *on earth as it is in heaven.* Everybody else is goin' the wrong way.

How hard it is to be a follower of Jesus, at least as I understand the message of his Gospel. How hard it is to be a peacemaker. How hard it is to love my enemy. How hard it is to be meek when all I see around me are strongmen (and they usually are *men*) and bullies running the world, and getting elected, reelected, and sometimes literally getting away with murder—or bragging that they could. They're the ones who seem to be winning, not the meek, not the poor, not the crucified. But because it's hard, that's exactly why it's prophetic.

And yet, I am a prisoner of hope, and the still small voice inside of me keeps whispering, "To everything there is a season." *Do not be deceived; God is not mocked,* Paul says in the Letter to the Galatians, which could be the New Testament response to Qoheleth: *You reap whatever you sow.* "To everything there is a season." And so, St. Paul says,

> Let us not grow weary in doing what is right, for we will reap at harvest time, if we do not give up. So then,

---

[10] Mt 7:24–27.

whenever we have an opportunity, let us work for the good of all, and especially for those of the family of faith.[11]

To everything there is a season. God will not be mocked. Chuang Tzu says, "From of old, nothing has ever won against Heaven." And our greatest example of this of course is Jesus, the anti-strong man who humbly accepted even death, death on a cross. This is what it means to be King of the Universe and Lord of Creation and to have dominion over the earth— to humbly accept becoming a servant to all, surrendering into the hands of his *Abba* who raises him from the dead and pours out the Spirit on all flesh—and *your sons and your daughters shall prophesy, your old men shall dream dreams, and your young men shall see visions.*[12] And, what's more, pours his love *into our hearts through the Holy Spirit that has been given to us*[13]—the Spirit of the Risen Christ.

I know that I'm an author and a recording artist and am somewhat well known for my work in the world. But at the end of the day, I think of myself as just a singer and a guitar player and a scruffy and not very bright monk. I do not have brilliant practical solutions to the problems facing our world. I don't know how to bring peace to the Middle East or how to resolve the immigration crisis or the best way to adapt to clean energy. But I do know that neither tyranny nor terrorism is a sustainable solution. And I am sure of this: Jesus really taught a different way to be in the world, from the micro to the macro. And I can think of nothing more prophetic than to preach the Gospel of Jesus. Nothing more radical, more countercultural, than to nurture and promote the values of the Spirit—love, peace, joy, patience, kindness, goodness,

---

[11] Gal 6:7–10.
[12] Jl 2:28–29.
[13] Rom 5:5.

gentleness, faithfulness as well as self-control—in little ways and great. I'm like Pete Seeger on this: It's the only kind of song I know how to sing.

Do you know what time it is in your life? Do we know what time it is in our life as a community, as a church? Well, I'll tell you what time it is: It's late, but it's not too late. Even if the Earth were about to melt down, even if civilization were poised on the brink of crumbling, even if we feel it's too late to do anything about our physical beings or our psycho-emotional growth, and no matter who is occupying 10 Downing Street, the Kremlin, the Knesset, or the White House, it's never too late for radical obedience to the teachings of Jesus. It's never too late to start taking the Gospels seriously, believing that its teachings actually work and that they can make the world a better place.

Then we would truly be prophetic.

9

Like a Mother

On What It Means to Be Church

A lot of people, myself included, tend to associate religion in general, and perhaps Christianity in particular, with scolding and finger-wagging. The caricature of that is the almost archetypal "church lady," like the character Enid Strict portrayed some years ago by the comedian Dana Carvey on *Saturday Night Live*.

In contrast, in recent years I have noticed Catholic Christianity becoming more and more associated with a kind of intellectual certainty, a fortress of objectivity and rationality in the midst of a swamp of relativity and uncertainty. This is a more apologetic approach to evangelization that defends the doctrines of the faith through argumentation. That's certainly a lot better approach, and more appealing, than the scolding church lady.

Several writers in turn have contrasted that particular approach to evangelization with Pope Francis's approach, who was known for trying to always lead with mercy. There is a charming emblematic anecdote told about Pope Francis, for instance, recounting a visit he made one time to an eighty-seven-year-old woman and the long conversation he had with her about her recipe for ravioli. What was notable about it was that Francis remembered so many little details about the woman and their encounter. It was very personal, a meeting of hearts more than a meeting of minds. That pretty much sums up his approach to evangelization.

Francis, of course, is also famous for saying to priests that "the shepherd should smell like the sheep." We lived just up the road from a sheep farm when I was a teenager, and I can say from personal experience that sheep can be pretty smelly. The photo that won the world over (and certainly won me over) on Holy Thursday 2013, right after he was elected, was of Pope Francis washing the feet of prisoners in Rome. Normally the pope would wash the feet of twelve clergymen in St. Peter's Basilica at the Mass of the Lord's Supper on that day. But this time it wasn't in St. Peter's, and it wasn't only done to priests. As a matter of fact, they weren't all men either. And they weren't even all Christians! It didn't win everybody over, however. This threw some liturgists into quite a tizzy, and it was right about then, right at the very beginning of his pontificate, that some voices—I'm not sure what adjective to use for them: "traditional"? "conservative"? "orthodox" voices?—started finding Francis a little smelly too. But I was reminded again of the story of Pope Paul VI who, when he opened the second session of the Vatican Council, challenged the council fathers to change their attitude toward the world: "Not to conquer but to serve; not to despise but to appreciate; not to condemn but to comfort."

Let's say one approach, the apologetic one, is more objective and the other is more subjective. One is *argument* and the other is *accompaniment*. (Some, who wonder if apologetics actually *is* evangelization, would say that one is apologetics and the other is actual evangelization.) I suppose we need a little of both approaches—and a lot less of the church lady—and the ability to know what is appropriate when, in any given situation.

More broadly speaking, it strikes me that one approach is very masculine and the other is feminine. We are not speaking here just about gender. I mean archetypally masculine and feminine, like the *animus* and *anima* of ancient spirituality, such as that of the eleventh- to twelfth-century Cistercian abbot William of St. Thierry, even before Jungian psychotherapy, or the *yin-yang* of Taoism, or the *ha-tha* (sun-moon) of classical Yoga, or the *shiva* and *shakti* of the Tantric tradition.

I want to rush in to say I certainly don't mean feminine like The Church Lady. I mean feminine like a mother.

Not that these approaches are mutually exclusive, but I often ask myself which approach does the world need from us right now, muscular and apologetic or personal and accompanying? Again, there is a time for both approaches. But here I want to make an argument in favor of the latter approach.

ॐ

One of the strongest of the rare feminine images we have of God in Scripture is the canticle from Isaiah 66. It's read three times throughout the church year in the Lectionary. It also finds its way several other times throughout the liturgical tradition as an antiphon and as a part of the Liturgy of the Hours, including being the canticle for Morning Prayer in the Roman Rite, Thursday of Week III. And it has a few verses in it that are enough to make a novice blush. I call it, "the Canticle of the Mother."

> Rejoice with Jerusalem, and be glad for her,
>> all you who love her;
> rejoice with her in joy,
>> all you who mourn over her—
> that you may nurse and be satisfied
>> from her consoling breast;
> that you may drink deeply with delight
>> from her glorious bosom.
> For thus says the Lord:
> . . . you shall nurse and be carried on her arm,
>> and dandled on her knees.
> As a mother comforts her child,
>> so I will comfort you;
>> you shall be comforted in Jerusalem.[1]

I think of this canticle as feminine not just because of its anatomical references, but also in that it is much more a message of comfort rather than of challenge. It's certainly not a message of rebuke as will often appear in other prophets, including the harsh words in earlier parts of the Book of Isaiah itself. (See, for instance, Isaiah 1:15: *When you stretch out your hands, I will hide my eyes from you; even though you make many prayers, I will not listen; your hands are full of blood. Wash yourselves; make yourselves clean.*) It's not completely clear in this Canticle of the Mother if and when Isaiah is referring to Jerusalem and when he is referring to God, but either way it's impossible not to see God portrayed as a mother here. It's quite startling, and it could come as a bit of a shock to some, to think of being nursed and comforted at God's abundant breast.

This Canticle of the Mother comes almost at the end of

---

[1] Is 66:10–13.

the very long book of the prophet Isaiah, and I think we understand it better when it's placed in the context of the rest of Isaiah's writing, especially the middle of the book that bears his name. After the early reprimanding voice of the first era, during the years 550–539 BCE an anonymous prophet, a disciple of Isaiah, rose up in the midst of the Hebrew exiles. He is usually referred to as Deutero- (or Second) Isaiah. Deutero-Isaiah's oracles are found in chapters 40 through 55, a section that is called the "Book of Consolation." Throughout this section, the prophet often speaks in double imperatives. As a matter of fact, it opens with the famous Advent words:

> Comfort, O comfort my people,
>   says your God.
> Speak tenderly to Jerusalem,
>   and cry to her
> that she has served her term,
>   that her penalty is paid,
> that she has received from the Lord's hand
>   double for all her sins.[2]

These poems of Deutero-Isaiah were very influential on the New Testament. As a matter of fact, after the psalms they are the most cited texts in the New Testament. Some scholars refer to this Book of Consolation as the favorite book of Jesus and his disciples. And we could get the sense that it contains much of the seed of Jesus' own theology.

Indeed, Jesus as portrayed in the Gospels seemed to spend a lot more time inviting than scolding, more time consoling than correcting. One of my favorite snapshots of Jesus in his ministry is in chapter 6 of the Gospel of Mark. Earlier

---

[2] Is 40:1–2.

in that same chapter we read that he had sent his apostles out on their first preaching mission, casting out demons and curing the sick. When they returned from that mission, they must have been excited to tell Jesus all that they had done and taught, and they were probably also bone tired. Mark tells us they had had no leisure even to eat. So Jesus invites them, in another famous line of Scripture, to *'Come away to a deserted place all by yourselves and rest a while.'* And so they go off in a boat headed to what they thought was going to be a deserted place. But a bunch of people saw them, recognized them, and *hurried there on foot from all the towns and arrived ahead of them.* When Jesus went ashore and saw the great crowd that had gathered waiting for them, we are told that, in spite of the apostles and perhaps he himself being tired and hungry—and this is the line I love—*he had compassion for them, because they were like sheep without a shepherd.*[3]

One of my monastic confreres preached on this vignette once and pointed out that in this particular scene Mark is showing us that Jesus' priority was always to allow the heart to speak above all. Jesus and the disciples would have been perfectly justified in having a day off, some time to celebrate their success in ministry together. But the right moment to love isn't set by those who love but by those who need love, not by us but by those who have need of us. In the monastic tradition this is known as *Caritas Ordinata*, "ordered love," a phrase that comes from the Scottish medieval philosopher and theologian Richard of St. Victor. It means that love always gives the precedence to those who have the most need, as Saint Benedict taught in his Rule for Monks that monks ought not ever pursue what is best for themselves, but what

---

[3] Mk 6:30–34.

they judge better for someone else.[4] Maybe especially in our day and age of self-help and recovery, we can often be so preoccupied with establishing our own legitimate priorities and healthy boundaries that we could end up totally losing sight of the example that comes to us from Jesus—to always give precedence to the needs of others.

And my confrere concluded by saying—and here is my point—that this is something that mothers know something about, because they are often grappling with a baby to whom they cannot do anything but respond. And Jesus was like a compassionate mother to this whole crowd: "Give them something to eat!"

Where we do see Jesus act in a more masculine way, if you will, is with the religious leaders of his time, the much-maligned scribes and Pharisees, among whom some were most probably very pious people. Or with the money changers in the Temple for whom he reserved his harshest act of civil disobedience, knocking over their tables and chasing them out with a whip, an act that was actually a challenge to the priestly caste too, many of whom were in cahoots with the Roman authorities. He condemns those who hurt others. For the poor, the sick, the little ones, the *anawim*, however, Jesus had compassion because they were like sheep without a shepherd. But even over those in power and those who were to reject his message, for whom the people of Jerusalem in general stand as an example, the city that *'killed the prophets and stoned those who were sent to her,'* Jesus lamented, saying that he wished he could gather her children together *'as a hen gathers her brood under her wings,'* but they were not willing.[5] Like a mother.

---

[4] RB 72:7.
[5] Lk 13:34–35.

What was Jesus' evangelization like? The message he sends his disciples out with in the Gospel of Luke is simply this: *'Peace be to this house! The reign of God is at hand for you.'* This comes even before repentance for the forgiveness of sins. *'Peace be with you! The reign of heaven is at hand.'* And if anyone does not welcome the disciples or this message, Jesus doesn't call down the fire of heaven and consume them as his apostle companions James and John would have him do later (and Jesus rebuked *them* for that!).[6] He simply wipes the dust of that town off his feet and moves on, and has his disciples do the same.[7]

John the Baptist had a fierce message preparing the way, with his declaring that there was already an *axe lying at the root of the tree,* announcing that the Messiah would have a *winnowing-fork in his hand to clear his threshing floor* and would *burn the chaff with unquenchable fire.*[8] If there is fire that Jesus calls down from heaven, it's the fire of the Holy Spirit—*'and how I wish it were already kindled!'*[9] he says. And his winnowing fan is *'Blessed are the poor in spirit!'* His axe laid to the root of the tree is *'Turn the other cheek.'*[10] It's sometimes easier to have a God who is Ruler/Judge, just like it's easier to have a religion that gives us all the black-and-white answers to our problems and intellectual conundrums. Then we don't have to think and decide for ourselves. A harsher thing is to have a God who is full of tender compassion. Then we have no one to blame. It's also easier when we think that the whole world is out to get us, when there's an assumption of malice and we have to batten down the hatches and protect ourselves

---

[6] Lk 9:51–56.

[7] Lk 6:5–11.

[8] Mt 3:10–12.

[9] Lk 12:49.

[10] Lk 12:49; Mt 5:3; 38.

against our enemies. The real challenge is when we realize that the whole universe is conspiring to our happiness, and '*the Father is glad to give you the kingdom,*'[11] as Jesus tells his listeners. Then the burden is on us, to accept it, to live up to the love that is being showered on us, to take the talents and use them as seed for the spreading of that same love throughout the world to every creature, to offer this same compassion to all those we meet, to be heralds of this Good News ourselves. To have compassion on the world, because they are like sheep without a shepherd.

Matthew quotes Jesus citing Hosea 6:6 two different times, *Go and learn what this means, "I desire mercy, not sacrifice." For I have come to call not the righteous but sinners.*[12] The Aramaic word for "mercy" that Jesus would have used is *rahamim*, which is quite close to the Hebrew word *rachum,* a word that describes what a woman feels toward the child she carries in her womb. We run into it in the Book of Exodus when we are told that *the Lord passed by in front of Moses and proclaimed, "The Lord, the Lord God, compassionate [*rachum*] and gracious, slow to anger, and abounding in lovingkindness and truth."*[13] If I may bring in yet another of the children of Abraham here, it's actually the same Semitic root as the Arabic word that begins every *surah* of the Qur'an in Islam, *Bismillah ir-rahman ir-rahim*—"In praise of Allah all merciful and compassionate" from the word *rachma*—mercy. The womb features strongly there too. *Rahim* is the Arabic word for "womb" and is also the second of the 99 Beautiful Names of God; the first of them is *Rahman*. My Muslim friends explain to me that *Ir-rahman* is the masculine manifestation of

---

[11] Lk 12:32.
[12] Mt 9:13; see also 12:7.
[13] Exodus 34:6.

mercy—the mercy of God that is vast and innumerable; and *al-Rahim* is feminine—the mercy God bestows on creation like a mother to a child. And as one friend said, "All creation is birthed from a *Rahim* of some kind."

❧

Years ago I read a screed (several have followed) against the great monastic Saint Bernard of Clairvaux, faulting him with being the one responsible for over-feminizing monastic spirituality because he wrote so many commentaries on the Song of Songs. (He wrote eighty-six sermons on it, and he only got to chapter 3!) He was one of the earliest exponents of what is known as bridal mysticism. Whereas the Jewish tradition understood the Song of Songs as referring to the marriage between God and the People of Israel, and the earliest patristic writings understood the Song to be between Christ and the Church, bridal mysticism understood the Song of Songs as being between God and the individual soul. And yet St. Bernard, even if he were guilty of emasculating spirituality, was still very much in the corridors of power and lent his authority to preaching in favor of the Crusades. This is what one of my acquaintances referred to as a "muscular Christianity," which I'm sure he meant as a compliment.

Francis of Assisi, in contrast, did not think that the Crusades were holy at all. In 1219 he took a companion, Brother Illuminatus, and set out to visit the Sultan of Egypt and Syria, Malik-al-Kamil, the nephew of the great Salah al-Din, unarmed and filled with love for his "enemy" brother, as St. Bonaventure wrote in his *Major Life* of St. Francis. They first went to the Christian camp, however, to meet with Cardinal Pelagius, the Christian commander, to beg him to stop the fighting. Pelagius refused. And so, in total disobedience to the good cardinal, the two friars crossed enemy lines and headed for Malik's camp. When they arrived there, the men of the sultan's army captured Francis and Illuminatus, and dragged them, beaten and exhausted, before the sultan—which of course was just what Francis wanted. To everyone's surprise, the sultan was open to meeting these two vagabonds. Some suggest that perhaps he thought they were Sufis, wandering dervishes.

Francis' was the softer approach, not the muscular one. Or at least a different kind of muscle: The Sultan of Egypt had decreed that anyone who brought him the head of a Christian should be rewarded with a Byzantine gold piece. That's some kind of courage!

Whereas Bernard of Clairvaux had preached and written urging Christians to "take up the cross" for a holy war against the infidels, in Saint Francis' first rule written in 1221, chapter 16 is titled "Missionaries among the Saracens and other Unbelievers,"[14] and in it he says there are two ways that the friars are to conduct themselves. The first way is to avoid quarrels or disputes and *be subject to every human creature for God's sake,*[15] and thus "[bear] witness to the fact that they are Christians." And only then comes proclaiming the word of God openly, "when they see that is God's will."

We are told by secondary sources that when Francis was with the sultan, he was careful to do nothing to insult the Prophet nor refute Islam. He simply preached the Good News. It was obviously effective. St. Bonaventure tells us, "When the sultan saw his enthusiasm and courage, he listened to him willingly" and pressed Francis to stay with him.

---

[14] "Saracen" is a medieval term used interchangeably for Arab and Muslim, from the old French, perhaps originally from the Arabic word for "east"—*sarki.*

[15] 1 Pt 2:13.

Along that same line (and I think we could safely say that St. Francis had a better relationship with his mother than with his father), when he wrote his Rule for Hermits, Francis instructed that "those who want to remain in a hermitage to lead a religious life should be three brothers, or four at most." Of those he wanted two of them to be "sons," and two, or at least one, to be "mothers."

∽

I grew up with the words "Holy Mother the Church" (with capital letters) emblazoned in my poor little conscience. It conjured up a rather huge and fierce image for me. But I had to re-think that image when I read Pope Paul VI's much-over-looked first encyclical *Ecclesiam Suam* from 1964. He wrote that the Church was founded by Jesus not only to be a min-ister of salvation, but first of all to be the "loving mother of the whole human family." The pope uses an interesting word in saying that "our attitude is entirely *disinterested*," meaning that he was, and the Church was, "devoid of any temporal or political motives." The sole purpose of the Church is to take whatever is already good in human life and "raise it to the supernatural and Christian level." And then he presents a model of concentric circles: first humankind in general, then worshippers of the one God, then Christians, then Catholics. And then he writes, "we find ourselves at the center," ready to meet and dialogue, humbly acknowledging, however, that the papacy itself is sometimes an obstacle.

What is somewhat prescient about that image of the con-centric circles is the use of a holarchy favored by many femi-nist theologians as opposed to a hierarchical model, some-thing that expands and includes rather than transcends and leaves behind. I thought of that too when I read what Pope

Francis said in Sicily in September 2018, which also serves as a counterpoint to all the talk of Christian Nationalism and Dominionism that is popular among so-called populist politicians. The Holy Father urged the clergy to "feel for the life of your people who are in need, listen to your people. This is the only populism possible," he said, and "the only 'Christian populism': to listen to and serve the people without yelling, accusing, and starting conflicts." Not an apologist, not a scolding church lady. More like a loving mother.

Of course, I would be horribly neglectful if I didn't mention Paul VI and Francis' predecessor Pope John XXIII, who set the tone in his famous opening address to the Second Vatican Council. In it he said that he disagreed with the "prophets of gloom" who were "always forecasting disaster, as though the end of the world were at hand." He decided that the world needed something other than "condemning errors with the greatest severity." Instead, the Spouse of Christ preferred to make use of "the medicine of mercy" and desired "to be the loving mother of all, benign, patient, full of mercy and goodness" even, perhaps especially, toward those who were separated from her and toward humankind in general that was (and still is) "oppressed by so many difficulties."

☙

I've noticed three different responses to the sex scandals that have been plaguing the Catholic Church since at least 2002. One is this very masculine, muscular approach: re-clericalize! Show Father skiing in his Roman collar (I actually saw this in a Catholic newspaper), shout down all detractors and prove that we're right, with a zillion followers on social media. Another response has been despondency, despair, depression, the temptation to leave the whole darned thing behind, as many have.

A third way, which may be the middle way between fight and flight, is to go down with Jesus into the Paschal Mystery and be the face of comfort, the voice of peace, the hands of service, not the Church Triumphant or the Church Militant, but the Church Penitential. And hopefully rise up from out of the ashes as the Church Servant, the Church Comforter, the Church that is known to be the "loving mother of the whole human family."

And so, I ask again: what is the face of church that we want to convey? What does the world need of us? Our faith is not a fortress of intellectual certainty and adherence to a set of propositions. It's first and foremost a *relationship*, like a mother to a child.

☙

There's a Buddhist practice that I learned years ago that has had a profound effect on me and that I have continued to use both in my personal prayer and in retreats I lead for years. It's called the *Metta* practice. *Metta* is an ancient Pali word that has all kinds of meanings. Often it is translated as "loving-kindness," but it can also mean "friendliness, goodwill, compassion," even "non-violence." The idea of the *Metta* practice is simple: at the end of a period of meditation you would dedicate whatever merit you might have gained from the practice out to others. That's why sometimes this tradition is also called the "dedication of merit." When our friend Reverend Heng Sure, who is a monk of the Chinese Ch'an Buddhist tradition, taught me his musical version of this *Metta,* Heng Sure added with a wink, "This is the Buddhist version of intercessory prayer." And so it has been an especially useful resource for me at interreligious gatherings (even if I do say under my breath, "and we make this prayer through Christ our Lord").

The way it was taught to me was that you're supposed to start with yourself first. Especially the folks I know in the Tibetan tradition always like to insist that it's okay for us to be happy too, we just aren't supposed to stop there. So we start out by saying, "May I be well, may I be happy, may I be at peace." And then we start widening the circle to all the people in the room whom I have meditated with, and even picture them in your mind or look around and see their faces: "May all these folks be well, may they be happy, may they be at peace." Then we just keep broadening the circle wider and wider, to all creatures on this land; to all the people in the area: "May they be well, may they be happy, may they be at peace." Then farther and farther yet, maybe to all people in my state, across my country: "May they all be well, may they be happy, may they be at peace." When I lead this practice, I always like to throw in a shout-out to the Gospel of Jesus at this point and suggest that folks pray for their so-called enemies, someone they are angry with, someone on the other side of the political aisle or ideological spectrum: "May they be well, may they be happy, may they be at peace." And then for all the war-torn parts of the world, for the hungry and poor, dedicate merit to our enemies foreign and domestic. And then, though this is the part that I thought was silly when I first heard it and it took me a while to get used to it, from my little heart I dedicate whatever merit I might have gained to all sentient beings anywhere throughout the cosmos. Here I remind myself of St. Paul's notion in the Letter to the Romans that *all creation is groaning* while we work out this redemption of our bodies.[16]

At the end of the practice a "prayer" of sorts is said together.

---

[16] Cf. Rom 8:22.

Every Buddhist school seems to have its own version of it, and I have collected many of them. My favorite comes from San Francisco Zen Center and Tassajara Zen Mountain Center with whom our monastic community has had a long friendship for decades. It ends with the words: "Even as a mother protects with her life her only child, so with a boundless heart should we cherish all living beings."

For my taste, this is what our attitude toward the world should be like too, like a "loving mother of the whole human family," cherishing all living beings. Which is only in imitation of God's attitude toward us, as God tells us through the prophet Isaiah: *As a mother comforts her child, so I will comfort you.*

10

The Wealth
of the Nations

On Interreligious Dialogue

Just after he was elected, the new prior general of our monastic congregation came from Italy to America for an official
visitation of our community in California. During his stay
with us he offered a conference to all the monks in which
he gave us some insights into the Church in Europe. At one
point he referred to a wave of xenophobia that he said was
washing through the continent with all the immigration that
was happening at the time. He told us that some people in
Italy were referring to this as a new "barbarian invasion."
And I asked him, how did the Church feel about this? And
he said the European Church too was quite troubled by this
"invasion." And the religious? He said sadly that he thought
that even religious were being affected by this attitude. And
us? *"Noi invece, amiamo i barbari,"* he said: "We love the
barbarians." I laughed out loud at that, with delight.

That was the period when I was living away from my
community, up near Santa Cruz, California, and had a lot

of interaction with folks outside of the visible confines of the Church. After the conference he was coming toward me to ask me something, and as he drew near, I said to him jokingly, *"Anch'io sono un barbaro!"* "I'm a barbarian too. I live with the barbarians! I'm like the abbot of the barbarians!" And he looked me dead in the eye, pointed his finger at me and said, in Italian, "That's exactly why we need you." I must say, I had never felt so honored, so seen, so valued in my vocation as I did in that moment. And I knew I had joined the right congregation of monks.

∽

As part of recounting the story of Jesus' birth, the Gospel of Matthew informs us that shortly after Jesus was born some *wise men from the East came to Jerusalem, asking, 'Where is the child who has been born king of the Jews?'*[1] There are several lessons we can glean from that event, commonly known as "the visit of the Magi." First of all, these are foreigners, assumedly not from the Chosen People of Israel, so we are getting a first hint that in the Christ-event the Gentiles are to become *fellow-heirs, members of the same body, and sharers in the promise in Christ Jesus through the gospel,* as Paul wrote in the Letter to the Ephesians.[2] The prophet Isaiah especially, who scholars tell us had a strong influence on the ministry of Jesus as well as on his self-understanding, had dreamed of this day. In chapter 49 of the Book of Isaiah, for example, God says through the voice of the prophet, *'It is too light a thing that you should be my servant to raise up the tribes of Jacob and to restore the survivors of Israel.* That's not enough! *I will give*

---

[1] Mt 2:7–12.
[2] Eph 3:6.

you as a light to the nations, that my salvation may reach to the ends of the earth.'[3] Isaiah says again later in chapter 60 that *'the nations shall come to your light.'*[4] And here it is starting to happen. Remember how already in the infancy narratives of the Gospel of Luke there are hints of this as well when we are told that old Simeon in his song when Jesus is presented in the Temple says specifically and prophetically, *'my eyes have seen your salvation, . . . a light for revelation to the Gentiles.'*[5]

Good for the Gentiles! The covenant has broken out of its container in ethnic Judaism. And these foreigners have come to worship this child Jesus, bringing gifts. Good for the Gentiles!

And then one day I suddenly realized, wait a minute. . . . Not only am I a barbarian; I'm also a Gentile! We're *all* Gentiles! That's all of us. It's true that Jesus instructs his first disciples to limit their ministry to the *'lost sheep of the house of Israel,'*[6] though I think the accent is on the "lost" not on "Israel"—go to the *lost* sheep of the house of Israel. And yet Jesus himself is often seen with, ministering to, and praising people outside the narrow confines of his co-religionists. He had a love for all those who get left out, squeezed out, all those who fall off the boat, those who are under the radar. And that too begins here with the visit of these foreigners.

From the beginning Jesus was always seeking out the lost ones. *He had compassion on them*—how I love this line—*because they were like sheep without a shepherd.*[7] How many times I thought of that line, walking down Water Street in Santa Cruz, passing the courthouse and the jail and the AA drop-in

---

[3] Is 49:6.
[4] Is 60:3.
[5] Lk 2:32.
[6] Mt 10:6, 15:24.
[7] Mt 9:36, Mk 6:34.

house, the homeless people camping out on the riverbanks and the New Age hippie kids dancing in the plaza. And I'd think to myself, "They're like sheep without a shepherd." There's a line from a wonderful song called "Come All You Weary" by a singer-songwriter named Dustin Kensrue: "Come all you weary, move through the earth / You've been spurned at fine restaurants and kicked out of church." I think it's brilliant to put those two images together, because so many of our churches and religious communities carry much more the spirit of fine dining and polite company than the company of drunks, tax collectors, lepers, and prostitutes. Many of our spiritual communities carry much more the smugness of chosen ones instead of Gentiles, the pure ones instead of barbarians.

But there's a further implication to this story. Yes, the three wise men coming to visit this child, bearing their gifts, are symbols of the rest of the world, of spiritual seekers outside of the Hebrew covenant entering the promise, and of the revelation which first came to the Jewish people breaking out of its container. But the uniqueness of this event is not just in their visit. It's also in the fact that they had their gifts to bring too. Not only that: their gifts were received and accepted. They came bringing their treasures, and their treasures were received, along with their uncircumcised flesh. And just so, when people come to Christ or come to the church, they don't have to leave everything of themselves behind nor the treasures that they have found in far-flung lands. Who they are, what they have to offer is welcome because—as St. Thomas Aquinas taught—grace does not destroy but builds on nature. Who we are is fine, as long as we come to God, as long as we allow all that we are and all that we have to be baptized and converted. And that opens this argument up a little more.

There are different theologies of and approaches to inter-religious dialogue. The most conservative is the theology of replacement, which means one religion just comes in and completely wipes out the other. But Catholicism (I do not want to speak for other branches of Christianity) is firmly rooted in the fact that "grace builds on nature." So we do not teach a theology of replacement, though sadly I must say that we did operate out of that way of thinking in our missionary work for centuries. The mainstream view is a theology of *fulfillment*, which means that all other religious traditions are brought to their fulfillment in Christ, not wiped out by him. And so, as the late Jesuit Jacques Dupuis put it, other religions are not just *pre*-Christian; they can be seen as *pro*-Christian, pointing to Christ in some way. That was the point of view of even such a stalwart of Christian orthodoxy as G. K. Chesterton concerning both philosophers and sages such as Confucius and the Buddha: What they intuited is brought to its fulfillment in the Christ event. As Pope John Paul II wrote, the seeds of truth that are present and active in the various religious traditions are all a reflection of the unique Word of God, who enlightens everyone coming into the world and who became flesh in Christ Jesus.[8] "They are together an 'effect of the Spirit of truth operating *outside the visible confines of the Mystical Body*' and which 'blows where it wills.'"[9] We might say that other religions, like these visitors from the East, have their treasures to bring, and gifts to offer which should be accepted.[10]

---

[8] Cf. Jn 1:9, 14.

[9] Cf. Jn 3:8; John Paul II, General Audience, September 9, 1998.

[10] Besides this careful theology of fulfillment, which some say is still too confining, there are some more liberal and progressive theologies of inter-religious dialogue. There is, for instance, the theology of mutuality—there are many true religions which are called to dialogue—and the theology of acceptance—there are many religions which actually have different ends completely.

And these three wise men from the East serve as a poignant image for that way of thinking. They come bringing gifts that they aren't told to leave at the door. Their treasures are laid at the feet of Jesus, and they are accepted. They don't just come to receive; they come bringing gifts, and their gifts are welcomed.

Now I want to take that even one step further by means of a story. When I was passing through Delhi, India, several years ago, I visited a monastic community known as the Brotherhood of the Ascended Christ that belongs to the Church of North India, the Indian version of Anglicanism. Their monastery is where Abhishiktananda stayed often on his way through Delhi and is also the place where his scant archives are housed. The head of the Brotherhood at the time was also the secretary of the Abhishiktananda Society. We had a long conversation during which he told me how influential Abhishiktananda had been on their community. We spoke about where and how to find a bridge with other traditions, and what to do about not just the uniqueness of Christ but the Christian insistence on the centrality and necessity of Christ for salvation, something which is often a real stumbling block in interreligious dialogue. (Hence also the negativity around even the theology of fulfillment.) I mentioned how I always fall back on a theology of the Word, meaning that wherever we discover Truth, Beauty, or Goodness we are already encountering the Word, the Second Person of the Trinity, who, we believe, was made flesh in Jesus who is the Christ, which goes right in line with this theology of fulfillment.

At that point this monk got very animated and told me how much Abhishiktananda's theology of the Word had influenced the whole Church of North India, so much so that they practically quote him in their Eucharistic Prayer: "From age to age you sent wise men and women to show us the way to you." He said any Indian would know that the rishis of India and the Buddha and the Jains and the Sikhs are all included in that phrase. So there's this beautiful example of laying gifts at the feet of Jesus and him accepting them; they already had something to offer. This man spoke about Abhishiktananda's understanding of "bringing the wealth of the nations to Christ," treasures such as the truth of the experience of nonduality or the wisdom gathered from such spiritual practices as yoga and Buddhist-style meditation.

But then he went a step further and explained what more that had meant for Indian Christians, that Abhishiktananda might not have realized. The monk I was speaking with, as many especially Protestant Christians, was a *dalit*, that is, he was of the "untouchable" caste. And he said, "For myself, as a *dalit*, not only do we bring the wealth of the nations to Christ, but then Christ distributes the wealth of the nations back to us!" He went on to explain how there was a time when the *dalits* were not allowed into Hindu temples because they would pollute the place and the Brahmin priests. He told me about an image that is used among Christians, "the drum of the Word," which refers to the ironic fact that because Brahmin priests could not have contact with animal skin, they could not beat the drum that was necessary for certain rituals. So they had to get a *dalit*, an untouchable to do it for them from a distance. "So you see," he said, "the *dalits* have been beating the drum of the Word all along."

And this, he said, is the tension between the Christian priesthood and the Brahminical one: the Brahmins, at least at one time, were not allowed to touch the *dalits* or have anything to do with them. Whereas, this man said, "I have been to many Roman Catholic ordinations, and it says specifically in the rite that they have the power to sanctify, the duty to touch the so-called unclean, and they will actually lay their hands on them. Christian priests say, 'You come and I will bless you.'" He said this was the same tension between the priesthood of Aaron and the priesthood of Melchizedek that Abhishiktananda loved to point out: the priesthood of Aaron would not allow itself to be polluted by unholy things, but the priesthood of Melchizedek, the line in which Jesus was a priest according to the Letter to the Hebrews, is the cosmic priesthood that sanctifies the wealth of the nations for Christ. And then Christ distributes that wealth to everyone, which means a *dalit* like the monk I was speaking with—and this was the mind-blowing point—didn't get the wealth of India from Hinduism; he got the wealth of India from Jesus. He gets the brilliant depths of Indian philosophy and practices such as yoga and meditation, everything, from Jesus who has gathered the wealth of the nations, the fullness of the Word, wherever it has manifested, and then spreads it out to everyone with bliss bestowing hands.

I want to add that this is not isolated to Christianity. The Hindu guru of the center where I did my yoga training assumed for himself too the right to train *pujaris* who were not of the Brahmin caste. But that was one of the most beautiful examples I have ever heard about the place of Christ in this whole economy of cosmic salvation, as well as the role of the Church. As St. Paul says, and now this good news of reconciliation he has entrusted to us.[11] This is also the dynamism, you might even say the choreography of the Eucharist. Like the three wise men, we lay our gifts—our lives and our loves, our sorrows, our joys, our talents—at the feet of Jesus, on the altar; and they are lifted up, consecrated, and then given back to us, accepted, consecrated. To realize this is a real epiphany,

---

[11] Cf. 2 Cor 5:19.

that who we are and what we have to offer is already good and acceptable. *Grace upon grace.*

I know I will never get many people to confess that all things are brought to their fullness in Jesus Christ. But I will stand by this truth in any crowd: that when we put things in proper order, when we begin everything and anything by establishing right relationship with the Divine, then everything finds its fulfillment in incarnation, in the Word being made flesh.

∽

There's a great lesson here that we still need to learn as a Church. The good news is always breaking out of the containers that we construct to hold it, just as it broke out of the container of Judaism. How many people get left out of our staid, polite, safe spiritual communities, because we think they are barbarians or Gentiles or pagans? And they are like sheep without a shepherd. If we don't shepherd them, if we don't feed them when and where they are hungry, they will go off to someone else who will feed them. If we don't welcome their gifts, they'll go off to other churches, ashrams, zendos, Sufi circles, and get fed, and sometimes fed well. They also may go off to places where they get fed poison because we were too concerned with preserving some kind of a pure ethic or a pure cult or culture rather than being enriched by the gold, frankincense, and myrrh that the Gentiles and barbarians and pagans are carrying with them, sometimes in alabaster jars, sometimes in earthen vessels, sometimes in silk purses, sometimes in beat-up backpacks. And we will be all the poorer for not having incorporated the gifts that they have to offer our churches and our communities.

So we might ask ourselves, who are the people we consider barbarians? Gentiles? When running for president against Donald Trump, Hillary Clinton said at one point that half of Trump's supporters were a "basket of deplorables" because they were "racist, sexist, homophobic, xenophobic, Islamophobic." In other words, barbarians. That might have been the moment she lost the election because that's the moment she left out the Gentiles and barbarians. To her they were the Gentiles and barbarians, but not to Jesus. He invites them too to be co-heirs of the Reign of God. Or maybe it's those whom we don't think pass the litmus test of what we understand orthodoxy to be or whatever our own version of theological correctness or traditional values is, and we dismiss them out of hand as if they had nothing to offer us and we had nothing to talk about with them. We do so at our peril, because whenever we exclude anyone else from the Church, from the Table, from our embrace, we have actually excluded ourselves from the Reign of God.

It's not that the Reign of God doesn't have its own demands even after we are welcomed. But aside from loving God with our whole heart, soul, and mind, first and foremost of those demands is *love your neighbor as yourself.* Before everything else we offer other Gentiles the same welcome that has been offered to us, and we wash the feet of the other barbarians in the same way ours have been washed. We are to act with respect and kindness and generosity to all we meet, in the name of Jesus, "the King of all the Gentiles and desired one of all."[12]

---

[12] O antiphon for December 22.

11

The End
and the Goal

On the True Self

Those who know how to live
can walk abroad without fear of rhinoceros or
    tiger.
They will not be wounded in battle.
In them rhinoceroses can find no place to thrust
    their horn,
tigers can find no place to use their claws,
    the sword nowhere for its point to go. Why?
Because there's nowhere in them for death to
    enter.

—Tao te Ching #50

I was speaking with a friend one day while we were walking together on the beach, and at some point he got to talking about caterpillars turning into butterflies. The process is fascinating. The metamorphosis begins when the caterpillar spins a little silk pod called a chrysalis. Once the body is entirely wrapped in that, the caterpillar's body actually starts to digest itself, from the inside out, until all that remains is a bunch of liquid goop. What used to be a body gets broken down into what are called "imaginal cells," undifferentiated cells that can then become any kind of cell. Some cells turn into wings, some into legs, antennae, new organs.

Now as only scientists can figure out how to do, researchers were able to attach some kind of electrical impulse to some caterpillars and then again to them later when they had become butterflies, and subject them to a certain kind of stimulation before and after. What they discovered is that the butterfly had the same reaction to the stimulus that the caterpillar had had before, speculating that, despite dissolving into liquid goop, there is some kind of essential identity to the caterpillar that remains in the butterfly. (Is it a form of consciousness?) And my friend said excitedly, "This is not just a metaphor. This is how life really works!" Things sometimes completely dissolve until what seems like nothing remains of the self, and then it transforms into a new self.

☙

There is a framing device that I use often in various contexts for various purposes. I find it useful to distinguish between the *scopos* and the *telos*, that is, the goal and the end, of the spiritual life. This distinction is found in the writings of John Cassian, the great fourth-century chronicler of the desert monastic tradition. He and his friend Germanus went from their home in Palestine to Egypt to engage in a long series of conversations with the old men (*gerens*) of the desert, conversations that are passed down to us in a literary work called *The Conferences*. Their very first recorded conversation with "the most experienced of fathers of the monks" is with Abba

Moses, who points out to them that every art and discipline has both a *scopos* and a *telos*. These are Greek words meaning "a goal" (*scopos*) and "an end" (*telos*). You might think of them as the proximate (goal) and the ultimate (end). For farmers, for instance, the *goal* is to cultivate the land and till the soil toward the *end* of having a rich harvest and an abundant crop. A good modern example might be any kind of sporting event: the goal (*scopos*) is to score points ("to make a goal"), but the end (*telos*) is to actually win the game. If I can be excused a militaristic image, the famous adage applies here: You could win the battle (i.e., reach a certain goal) and still lose the war (the end you were really seeking). Of course, it goes without saying that this makes us discern carefully where we are willing to invest our energy. In addition, it is essential to understand what our end is since it might affect the goal we are striving to reach.

And Abba Moses explains to them that the monastic profession too has both a *scopos* and a *telos*, a goal and an end. When he asks Cassian and Germanus, "What is your goal and what is your end?" they say that they "bear all things for the kingdom of God." Indeed, Abba Moses says, that is the end, but you need a goal first. Poor Cassian and Germanus can't figure out what that goal might be. So he tells them: "The end (*telos*) of our profession . . . is the kingdom of God . . . but the goal (*scopos*) is purity of heart." In other words, in order to realize the reign of God we need to first of all cultivate purity of heart, which in any case is something more concrete to strive for.

One day it occurred to me that this could be very helpful in the area of interreligious dialogue. Despite the fact that a lot of people like to say, "It's all the same!" in reference to other religions, my experience is that the more I study other traditions outside of my own, the more I realize that we have to admit that we actually describe the *telos,* the ultimate end, in different ways, with different poetry, shall we say. And, as much as I am deeply committed to finding the ground we share between our traditions, I think the differences need to be respected and not simply glossed over.

And my favorite example of this revolves around the notion of the self.

Many Westerners tend to speak of "the East" in global terms, without acknowledging the differences among the various Asian religious-philosophical traditions. I am going to oversimplify here for the sake of brevity (and to avoid a deep scholarly discussion), but I think it's safe to summarize the three major Asian traditions as follows. (These three traditions are thought to have taken their classic form in an era known as the Axial Period, around five hundred years before the so-called Common Era, which begins with the birth of Jesus.)

Of the six classical philosophies (*darshanas*) of India, it is the *Advaita Vedanta* tradition, as transmitted in the Scriptures known as the Upanishads and articulated by the eighth-century philosopher Shankara, that seems to have really captured the imagination of Westerners and worked its way into our vocabulary, consciously or not. So I will limit myself to this one school of Indian thought. (There is not necessarily agreement even among those various other *darshanas* of India, by the way.) *Advaita* means "not two," hence this is a "nondual" tradition, referring to the human person and God—they are "not two."

Ultimate Reality according to this tradition can be described as the Ground of Being—*brahman*; and Ultimate Reality is also the Ground of Consciousness—*atman*. And the great discovery/realization of the Upanishads is that the Ground of Consciousness and the Ground of Being are "not two." In other words, if we were to take the interior journey to the ground of our own individual consciousness, we would discover our identity with the Ground of Being and be able to say, *"Ayam atma Brahman!"* "I am Brahman!" My real self is the great Self (with a capital "S" in English). Hence the Self-Realization Fellowship, so popular in the West since the early twentieth century, is all about this discovery of the true self who/which is in reality the Great Self—*Paramātmā.* But this does not mean that I (Cyprian) am God; it means that my self *(jivatman)* has disappeared into the Great Self *(Paramātmā),* "like a drop disappears into the ocean," as the famous saying goes. There is only Brahman, only God.

I remember the first time I read that last phrase and what a powerful impression it made on me. "Yes, that feels right to me!" I thought. "Eventually I am going to disappear into God like a drop into the ocean."

However, you can hardly get around the fact that one of the marks of existence for the Buddha is *an-atta,* the word in the ancient language of Pali (which the Buddha spoke) for "no atman"! No self! This is a departure from the typical Indian thought of that time, though just a step away from *Advaita Vedanta.* (I was actually confirmed in this by seeing a film of the Dalai Lama speaking to a gathering of Hindu monks, and he teased them saying, "You say, *atman,* and we say, no *atman!*" But then he laughed and added, "It does not matter!" He also spoke about this when I heard him speak live.) If there be a self, it is a *process.* The self is made up of what are called *skandhas,* heaps of aggregates, but they too are in a constant state of flux. There is no permanent abiding self of me or you or of God or the dog or the tree or chocolate or of anything. There is only "dependent co-arising," as the late popular Vietnamese Buddhist teacher Thich Nhat Hanh loved to point out: "This is because that is. This is not because that is not. This is born because that is born. This dies because that dies." *There are no eternal substances,* neither within us nor within the world. All there is, is impermanence. There's no ground! There is no atman! The thirteenth-century founder of the Soto Zen school of Buddhism, Dogen Zenji, invents the phrase in Japanese *mujo-bussho*—"impermanence-Buddha nature." Buddha nature is impermanence.

Again, I remember the exact day when I was reading the writings of Dogen on Bus 72 in Santa Cruz, California, when I actually grasped this concept, and I had a kind of ecstatic experience. "That's it! It's all impermanence! And suffering is caused by clinging to anything and hoping it will be permanent. What liberation!"

I want to add a tradition that gets spoken about less often, but one from which I have drawn immense consolation and insight, and that is the Taoist tradition of China, particularly as articulated in its greatest figures, the semi-historical figure Lao Tzu, who legendarily compiled the classic text the Tao te Ching, and a second great figure, Chuang Tzu, who left behind much more written work. Side note: I have been several times surprised and a little disappointed at how few people of Chinese background in Asia have read either of these mystical poetic philosophical works which have meant so much to me. Most people who identify as Taoists mainly practice a mixture of shamanism and some form of ancestor worship. But the ancestor worship actually points to an ambiguity about this tradition in regard to the self.

My favorite (and grossly oversimplified) way of understanding the Taoist tradition is that there is a generative emptiness at the heart of the cosmos, referred to as the "uncarved block" or the great Tao (usually translated as "the Way") that cannot be named, which is also called a "Great Mother" because it gives birth to "the ten thousand things." And note the tension in that phrase: It is an *emptiness* that is also a *fullness*, a void that is also a womb of all possibility. One could get the impression that the self is simply one of the infinitely variegated forms that emanates from that generative emptiness only to return to it, and many interpret it that way. However, Chuang Tzu's conception of the Tao does not necessarily entail a denial of the self in the same way that Buddhism does. The practice of ancestor worship, for instance, is based on the belief that deceased family members continue to exist after death, that their spirits can look after the family.

I came to Taoism later than Buddhism or Hinduism. But I eventually found myself referring to the mystical poetry of the Tao te Ching more often than that of either of the other traditions.

Now, these are all beautiful poetic descriptions of a profound mystical experience, and I can see how someone would come to any of those conclusions. But this is not Christian language! Despite the poetry of our mystics, we cannot get around this essential point of our faith: The moral of the story of the resurrection is that the self is not annihilated, even by the death experience! Actually, even further, the point of the story (which we can't get into at length here but is even more shocking in its implications) also seems to be that *even the flesh* shares in the glory in some marvelous way. Hence all the stories of the glorified body of Jesus. As the great Scripture scholar N. T. Wright always insists, many Christians do not even realize that the end (the *telos*) according to Christian Scriptures is not just for me to die and my soul to go to heaven. The end according to Scripture is *a new heaven and a new earth;*[1] the end is eschatological reintegration.

Many Christians have been so enraptured by the language

---

[1] Is 65:17; 2 Pt 3:13; Rev 21:1.

of Asian philosophy that they are often tempted to dismiss their own Christian description of the *telos* and casually assume that if our mystics really knew what they were talking about, they might have said the same thing that Shankara or Dogen had said. But I must say that I have grown to resent that attitude. No, I think we need to trust the spiritual intuition of our own mystics. Even though our language gets so close to the language of "no self," even in Scripture—Saint Paul says, *it is no longer I who live but Christ who lives in me* and *You have died, and your life is hidden with Christ in God*[2]—there's still a self there in a marvelous relationship with the Divine. Jesus woke up from the death experience in a whole new marvelous relationship with the One whom he called *Abba*, Father, and we are invited to share in that. And of course the mystics of Judaism and especially the mystics of Islam have stunningly beautiful love poetry regarding this abiding loving relationship.

So we, between our traditions, describe the *telos* in different ways.

But to my amazement, and relief, what we find out is that we actually describe the *scopos*, that proximate goal, in similar terms. Let me offer some examples, again revolving around the subject of the self. I ran into this beautiful phrase that I think is a wonderful, brief, and universal description of the goal (*scopos*) of the spiritual life: "To learn oneself is to forget oneself." Before I tell you where that comes from, let me give you some other examples from various traditions.

Jesus in Matthew 10:39 (among other places)[3] says: *'Those who find their life will lose it, and those who lose their life . . . will find it.'* I know for a fact that I am not the only one to

---

[2] Gal 2:20; Col 3:3.
[3] Mt 16:25; Mk 8:35.

find this from the Tao Te Ching #7 to be as close an iteration
as possible to Jesus' teaching:

> The wise put themselves last,
> and thereby find themselves first . . .
> abandon themselves and are thereby fulfilled.

This is echoed by Lao Tzu's successor Chuang Tzu:

> The perfect have no self;
> the spiritual have no achievement;
> the true sage has no name.

Here is something from one of the Upanishads of India, the
Katha:

> By study of the yoga of the self,
> the wise know that which is hard to see,
> that which is deeply hidden,
> which lies in the cave of the heart
> and rests in the depths, the ancient deity—
> and pass beyond joy and sorrow. . . .
> Drawing out that which belongs to *dharma*,
> they attain the subtle one and are exceedingly
>   glad
> for they have found the source of all
>   happiness.

This is from another beloved and much more popular sacred
text of India, the Bhagavad Gita, Chapter 4:

> All the actions get dissolved entirely
> of those who are free from attachment

and have no identification and no sense of
   mind with the body,
whose minds are established in the knowledge
   of the Self.

Islamic mystics have written in a way that is very dear to the
heart of Christian contemplatives, being based as we are in
the belief in the oneness of God. This is from the writings of
the Sufi mystic Abu Hamid al-Ghazali:

You are created by two things.
One is your body and your *zahir*–your outer
   appearance,
which you can see with your eyes.
The other is your *batin*–your inner forces.
This is the part you cannot see,
but you can know with your insight.
The reality of your existence is in your
   inwardness.
Everything is a servant of your inward heart.

Or, better yet, the Sufi master al-Bistami's pithy phrase:
"Forgetfulness of self is remembrance of God." And the first
one I mentioned was from Master Dogen himself:

To learn the Buddha Way is to learn one's self.
To learn one's self is to forget one's self.
To forget the self is to be actualized by myriad
   things,
when actualized by myriad things,
your body and mind as well as the bodies and
   minds of others drop away.

How I would summarize this is that what our traditions seem to agree on is the goal, the necessity of going beyond the small self. Islam refers to this small self as the *nafs,* and that, incidentally, according to a famous *hadith* or saying of the Prophet Muhammad, is the great *jihad,* the *jihad al-nafs,* the conquering of the self. That term is also used in the Arabic translation of the New Testament. In 1 Peter 4:18, the word *jahada,* the root of *jihad,* is used to describe one's internal struggle: "If it is *jahada* (struggle) for the righteous to be saved, what will become of the ungodly and the sinner?" We are looking to go beyond what we usually identify as the self, to experience this deeper reality, which perhaps we could call, along with Thomas Merton, our "true self," or our spirit, what Buddhists call Buddha nature, and an *advaitan* would call the *Paramātmā.* What we *call* that Reality that lies beyond the small self lies in the realm of the *telos,* the end, which we articulate in different ways. But we do recognize a common *scopos*, the necessity of going beyond the phenomenal self to whatever-that-is.

I like to put together Thomas Merton's phrase with that same line from St. Paul's Letter to the Colossians that I quoted above—*for you have died and your life is hidden with Christ in God*—and phrase it this way: Our true self is hidden in God. Christians, of course, would add that our true self is hidden *with Christ* in God.

What can we draw from this? First of all, because of this agreement, on the *scopos*, this proximate goal, the necessity of going beyond the phenomenal self to whatever-that-is, I think we should spend a lot more time discussing that instead of wringing our hands over subtleties about the *telos*—which we are probably never going to agree on or convince each other about, and we can't, this side of death, know exactly anyway. Trying to explain, let alone convince, my Jewish and Muslim friends about the Trinity (which I would hazard to say most Christians don't really understand either) is like trying to convince me about reincarnation. "I'm sorry," I always have to say. "That is a profound intuition, but I simply don't believe the Universe works that way. And it is certainly not the teaching of orthodox Christianity. But let's not spend anymore time discussing that. Let's talk about how we pray or about how to be more charitable."

And that leads to my second point: Because we agree on the proximate goal—going beyond the phenomenal self, the self we experience in our day-to-day life, to the true self—we can also find common ground on a third element, what the ancients called *praxis*, or "practice," the practical exercises that lead us to that goal, however we describe the *telos*, the ultimate end. I have someone who may surprise you to back me up on that: Joseph Ratzinger, the future Pope Benedict XVI.

Back in 1989, the Congregation for the Doctrine of the Faith issued a "Letter to the Bishops of the Catholic Church on Some Aspects of Christian Meditation." It was roundly criticized by liberals for being too restrictive and lauded by conservatives (if noticed at all) for bringing some sound doctrine to all these suspicious Eastern practices. Be that as it may, as is my wont, I found a paragraph in it that totally supports the work I do in interreligious dialogue.

In chapter 5 on "Questions of Method" it points out that the majority of the great religions which have sought union with God in prayer have also pointed out ways to achieve that union. (That is a huge recognition in and of itself on the part of a very conservative tradition.) The document then goes on to say that just as the Catholic Church doesn't reject anything true and holy in other religions, neither should these ways be rejected out of hand simply because they are not Christian.

On the contrary, one can take from them what is useful "so long as the Christian conception of prayer, its logic and requirements are never obscured." The only thing I strongly dislike here is the word "achieve," as in "achieve union with God." Let's use another word: "realize," to become aware of and to make real our already present union with God.

That being said, I would say the same about my idea of the *scopos*: Other traditions that have sought to go beyond the phenomenal self to the "real self hidden in God" have also pointed out ways to realize that, and those ways are not to be rejected out of hand simply because they are not Christian. Rather, they can be explored and taken up as long as the Christian conception of this relation of the self to the Divine is never obscured. This has been why so many of us have explored the cosmology, ontology, and metaphysics, as well as the spiritual techniques, of Asia, which articulate this search in a fresh new way and embody it in practices that we have found very helpful, oftentimes, with all due respect, more helpful for those of us exploring the inner life of contemplative prayer than typical Western popular religious devotional practices.

I see the work, exploration, and study I have done of comparative religion as having both of these aims in mind: first of all to truly understand and then rearticulate in a fresh new way for new generations the Christian conception of all these things—prayer, the self, union with God; and second, to learn what is useful, practically, poetically, and philosophically from other traditions toward that end, with the additional gift of perhaps being able to articulate our own concept of these truths in a fresh new way for new generations with all the insights we have gained in the evolution of human consciousness, perhaps in ways that might never have occurred to us with our cultural limitations. For my meditation practice, I find inspiration in the Upanishads, the Bhagavad Gita, the Dhammapada, the Tao te Ching, and the writings of the Sufi mystics, with their descriptions of and advice on how to realize the true self.

As already mentioned, this *scopos* was an important and well-known theme of Thomas Merton's, the distinction between our true self and our false self. Our false self is the identity that we cultivate in order to function in society, our persona, we could even call it our mask. Whereas our real self is a deep and holy mystery, perhaps only known to God. There is a mystical allusion to this in the image of the "white stone" in the Book of Revelation.

> To everyone who conquers … I will give a
>   white stone,
> and on the white stone is written a new name
> that no one knows except the one who
>   receives it.[4]

Robert Inchausti summarizes this teaching succinctly: "The world cultivates the false self, ignores the real one, and therein lies the great irony of human existence: the more we make of ourselves, the less we actually exist." In *New Seeds of Contemplation* Merton wrote that this false self is an illusory person, the one "that I want to be but who cannot exist," the one about whom God does not know anything.

Now, that to me is an important threshold in the spiritual life, to have not just intellectual knowledge, but actual existential experiential certainty that, first of all, there is something beyond this phenomenal entity which I identify

---

[4] Rev 2:17.

as me. And, second, to realize how much I am conditioned, that is to say, limited by this phenomenal self. Bede Griffiths is often quoted as saying that he thought the goal of the spiritual life was not to destroy or kill the ego, but just to realize how much we are conditioned by it. And, third, to long to and strive to realize whatever-it-is that lies beyond this false self. And, again, by "realize" I mean both to become aware of it and to make it real.

For my own self, this is like a constant ache, to have caught a glimpse of this, my real self, to have had a taste of it, like the Beloved slipping behind the veil in the Song of Songs, and to long for that passing state to become a permanent trait. To be haunted, even taunted, in a sense, by the knowledge that for the most part I am not living, moving, and breathing from that deepest such-ness.

꙯

I once attended an international conference in South India. I was one of only two monks there, the rest of the attendees were sociologists, anthropologists, statisticians, and other academics from around the world. On a long taxi ride and on another long bus trip, I developed a friendship with a particularly remarkable mathematician and professor of computer science from Iran. We certainly discussed interreligious and intercultural matters, but we mainly bonded over music. A Muslim by birth, the mathematician's spirituality seemed to be more than anything embodied in the poetry of the great Persian poet Rumi. To the amusement of our fellow travelers, he was reciting or singing poems to me in Persian while we rode along, with his eyes closed, gesticulating in the air with his hand, and then translating for me and explaining the inner meaning of the words. One of the things he told me that Rumi had inspired in him was that whenever he met anyone new, he would ask them as soon as possible, "What is the meaning of life to you?" Imagine that being the beginning of an acquaintanceship! But this was his great fascination, how other people experienced the world and what they thought was the purpose of it all. And of course, inevitably we exchanged our views on that with each other as well. At the risk of sullying a deep intimate sharing with my intellectual categories, looking back I realize that neither of us by that point had to mention Jesus or Allah—the *telos*. We spent the time talking about the *scopos*, the goal of our lives, and were very much in accord.

Sad to say, this is the kind of mature and rich conversation that I can't always have with my Catholic/Christian brothers and sisters, but I can and have had with serious spiritual practitioners of any authentic spiritual tradition—however we describe the *telos*.

12

Pious Claptrap

On Authority and Love

I think that preaching, especially in a parish, is one of the most challenging things a priest or a minister does, and I have such great admiration for those who do it week in and week out—and sometimes day to day—for years. There are at least three reasons why I find it difficult. First of all, because I'm a communicator, and I really want people not only to listen to me but also to truly understand what I'm saying. So I work so hard to make the point as clear as possible even when it's something dense. (I know teachers can sympathize with that.) Second, I'm just not very good at faking things. I can't sell something I don't believe in. I have to really understand and accept it myself in order to pass it on. And third—and this is the most challenging one—as my father used to say, "Who you are speaks so loudly that I can't hear a word you're saying." When you stand in front of a group of people and preach, you're not just saying, "Do what I say"; you're saying, "Be like me! If you listen to me, you can be just like I am. You can have what I've got."

That last one is a notion from AA that I really like, by

the way, that is usually read at the beginning of meetings. It's on page 58 of the Big Book. Before the Twelve Steps are introduced, they say, "If you have decided that *you want what we have* and are willing to go to any lengths to get it . . ." and then the Steps are read. I remember the first time I literally said those words about someone was when I met Fr. Bede Griffiths or, I should say, when I observed him, mostly from a distance, as he was visiting our monastic community on his last visit to America as I was just entering the community. I watched him during evening meditation in front of the Blessed Sacrament, and I said to myself, "I want what he has." He had an authority about his being that spoke as loudly as his words, which were undoubtedly weighty as well.

Now to be fair, my mother, for her part, presented the other side of the argument. She would sometimes half-jokingly say, "Do as I say, not as I do." There's a truth there too. As a matter of fact, Jesus himself advocates something like this, not regarding himself, but regarding the scribes and Pharisees of his time. He railed against the fact that the scribes and Pharisees did not practice what they taught, and yet he still told the crowds and his disciples that, since they sit on Moses' seat, '*Do whatever they teach you and follow it*'; just '*Do not do as they do.*' The Twelve Step Program teaches something similar too: "Principles before personalities," meaning, as I understand it, there are some principles and standards that are still true and valid even if others have not yet lived up to them. Just because someone else, even someone you admire, has lost their sobriety, you need to stick to your side of the street and work your program. I used to tell my young friends in a similar vein, "I'm not always sure of myself, but I am sure of this *way*," meaning the spiritual path I was following and promulgating. It's working for me, and I have experienced growth and maturity. You may get ahead of me at some point, and good for you! But please don't give up on this path even if I fall behind from time to time. Principles before personalities!

Still, with due apologies to my mother, my point abides: The days are pretty much gone when someone can get unlimited authority based solely on their rank or position, their broad phylacteries and long fringes, their place of honor at banquets and the best seats in the synagogues (or churches)—and good riddance! No. People in our day and age are much slower just to accept authority based on an external title or initials or fancy costumes.

◌

A friend of mine and I used to talk often about "empty words," meaning things people say that have no real meaning behind them, banal platitudes. As James Carroll wrote, "We find all too often that the words we use are empty, running like rats' feet over broken glass." ("Our thoughts and prayers" is my current favorite bête noir in this regard, the only response our politicians seem to have as a response to mass shootings.) Psalm 41 too speaks of our enemies as the ones who *utter empty words, while their hearts gather mischief.*[1] We also speak of Satan and all his "empty promises" in our baptismal formula.

I also sometimes get the impression from "religious" people—and I get annoyed with myself when I fall into the same pattern—that in a conversation I am getting what I call "undigested glop," a mere parroting of pat answers and doctrinal teaching that has nothing to do with personal experience, not rooted in any kind of ownership, and so lacking authority. There is nothing intrinsically wrong with

---

[1] Ps 41:6.

pat answers or parroted doctrines, I suppose, especially at a young age when we are learning the language and concepts of religion and trying on different roles, personas, and masks, ways of speaking and interacting according to who we want to be and how we want to be seen in the world. At the same time, I think part of Jesus' ministry was specifically to do away with the undigested glop, the pat answers, and the easy solutions.

Empty words. Undigested glop.

Let me add to that one other image: So much of our religious language strikes me as mere claptrap. The word "claptrap" literally means something said to elicit applause, to trap someone into clapping. And the example most dictionaries give is "pious claptrap," as if that were the most typical kind of claptrap, just spouting off religious sounding ideas, trying to elicit Oos and Ahs. That's what a lot of religious language comes to sound like, if not empty words and platitudes that come from safe formulas instead of conviction, then pious claptrap.

∽

One of my all-time favorite Zen stories, and a good example of undigested glop, is called "One-Fingered Zen." An old Chinese master named Juzhi accepted a very young monk as his disciple, and this boy would sit by quietly and observe the master all the time. For instance, whenever someone would ask Juzhi the question, "What is the Buddha dharma?" Juzhi would simply hold up one finger. When Juzhi wasn't around, the boy would surreptitiously take his place and pretend like he was enlightening people in the same way, by holding up one finger. One day the master found out about it, and he called the young monk to himself and asked him, "What is Buddha Nature?" And the kid proudly held up the one finger, at which point Master Juzhi said, "That's not Zen. You might as well be a parrot!" And he took out a knife and sliced the young monk's finger off. Well, of course the kid ran off howling in pain. But as he was running off, Juzhi called his name out once more, and when the boy turned around, Juzhi held up one finger. And at that moment, so the story goes, the boy was instantly enlightened.

Now, mind you, I do not think that the teacher actually cut the boy's finger off; it is a tale told to make a point. In the collection *Zen Speaks*, the Chinese artist and writer Tsai Chih Chung explains that "what other people have come to understand intuitively can never become yours unless you come to understand it through your own efforts." The young monk was borrowing Juzhi's words, parroting; they were not coming from his own knowledge. But somehow when Juzhi cut the boy's finger off and called him back, that experience slam-dunked him so hard into the present moment, into reality, into awareness, as only pain can do, that when the Master once again gave him the one-fingered sign of Buddha dharma, he understood, because he was right there. He saw the reality about that which the teacher had been teaching.

Another scene comes to my mind. There's a marvelous moment in the movie *Walk the Line*, the story of the life of the legendary singer-songwriter Johnny Cash. He and his two friends are auditioning before the famous producer Sam Phillips of Sun Records in Memphis. They're in the middle of singing a kind of insipid, innocuous southern gospel song when Sam Phillips suddenly stops them and says, "I'm sorry. I can't market gospel no more. . . . Gospel like that doesn't sell." Johnny Cash asks, "Was it the Gospel or the way I sing it?"

SP: Both.

JC: Well, what's wrong with the way I sing it?

SP: I don't believe you!

JC: You saying I don't believe in God? . . .

SP: You know exactly what I'm telling you. We've already heard that song a hundred times, just like that, just like how you sing it.

JC: Well, you didn't let us bring it home.

And Sam Phillips pauses for a moment, and then he says,

> Bring it home? All right, let's bring it home. . . .
> If you was hit by a truck and you were lying out in that gutter dying, and you had time to sing one song, one song people would remember before you're dirt, one song that would let God know what you felt about your time here on earth, one song that would sum you up, you tellin' me that's the song you'd sing? That same . . . tune we hear on the radio all day. . . . Or would you sing something different, something real, something you felt? 'Cuz I'm telling you right now, that's the kind of song people want to hear, that's the kind of song that truly saves people. It ain't got nothin' to do with believing in God, Mr. Cash; it has to do with believing in yourself.

Johnny Cash says, "Well, I got a couple songs I wrote in the Air Force. You got anything against the Air Force?" Sam Phillips says, "No." And Johnny Cash says, "Well, I do," and then he breaks into the song "Folsom Prison Blues," the song that would become his first hit.

I know the words "believing in yourself" currently have a

vague air of suspicious feel-good self-empowerment to them, but let me tell you what that means to me. Obviously, this all has something to do with believing in God, but the next step in real belief is "bringing it home," believing in who I truly am, believing in who you are, believing in what we believe in. I remember once when I had to make a big decision and stand before someone very important and announce what I had decided, and I was very nervous about it—worried about the consequences, second-guessing my decisions, afraid of being afraid, nervous that the words wouldn't come out right. A friend of mine wrote to me and said, "You just need to stand on your own I AM, on the ground of your being and speak from there." I was reminded of Jesus saying, as recorded both by Matthew and Mark, '*Do not worry about how you are to speak or what you are to say; for what you are to say will be given to you at that time.*'[2]

And that to me is the very image of Jesus. I like to think that at his baptism (as Abhishiktananda taught) the Father passed the *I AM*, which was the very name of God, on to Jesus by saying to him, "You are! You are my son. You are my beloved." And when Jesus spoke, he spoke from that *I AM*. And people knew it! How often do we hear in the Gospels how the crowds were astounded at Jesus' teaching, for example at the end of the Sermon on the Mount, Jesus' most famous discourse. Why? Because, Matthew tells us, he *taught them as one having authority, and not like one of the scribes.*[3] Not empty words, undigested glop, or pious claptrap. No one had ever spoken like this, with this kind of authority! And *they were filled with awe, and they glorified God, who had given*

---

[2] Mt 10:19; Mk 13:11.
[3] Mt 7:28.

such authority to human beings.[4] They believed *in* him because they believed *him*. And he was believable because he knew who he was; he spoke from the I AM.

God did not give that authority to just one human being, however. Every translation I know of puts that sentence in the plural: *They were filled with awe, and they glorified God, who had given such authority to human beings.* Through Jesus God passes that kind of authority on to his followers, the authority to cast out demons, the authority to forgive sins, and the authority to announce the Good News. That same I AM is planted in us. It's, first of all, the law written in our hearts that the prophet Jeremiah and Saint Paul speak about. It's also our baptismal inheritance, having been baptized into the prophecy, priesthood, and royalty of Jesus the prophet, priest, and king. We need to find that in us, we need to believe in that in us, and then speak from that in us.

And not only do we need to *speak* with that authority; we also need to *listen* with that kind of authority. In this day and age, when so many people have abused their power, and with so many charlatans and so many caricatures of Christianity and pseudo-spiritualities floating around, it's okay to ask the hard questions. It's okay to trust our own intuitions and experiences and suspicions. The words spoken to your ear have to match the Word that's already planted in your heart. Those who are standing on their own I AM can take the hard questions and are not going to be shaken by our asking them.

There is a section from the Vatican II document on Divine Revelation, *Dei Verbum*, that offers a subtle innovative teaching. To put this in context, for centuries the Catholic Church had a certain hesitation about individuals reading Scripture without hierarchical supervision and interpretation, which

---

[4] Mt 9:8.

was largely a reaction against the Protestant reformers notion of *sola Scriptura*, "Scripture alone," as opposed to the Scripture and Tradition of Catholicism. *Dei Verbum* (#8) taught that the "Tradition that comes from the apostles *makes progress* in the Church," and that there is "*a growth in insight* into the realities and words that are being passed on." That's already kind of shocking for the Catholic Church to admit, that Tradition makes *progress* and that there is *growth* in insight in the Tradition, perhaps a legacy of John Henry Newman.

But what was even more surprising was how it says this progress and growth into insight comes about. Mind you, I was told that there is always a hierarchy in Vatican documents, and so it is important that the first way this growth and progress in insight comes about according to this document, before the hierarchy is mentioned, is through the "contemplation and study of believers who ponder these things in their hearts," and "from the intimate sense of spiritual realities which they experience." And only *then* does *Dei Verbum* mention "the preaching of those who have received, along with the right of succession in the episcopate, the sure charism of truth." Growth comes from intimate experience of spiritual realities, not just from scholars and theologians pronouncing from on high, but from out of the believers' hearts!

In the language of spirituality there's an intimate connection between the ear and the heart. Psalm 95 urges us. *If today you hear God's voice, harden not your hearts.*[5] It's like what Saint Benedict says right at the beginning of the Rule for Monks: *Obsculta! Listen! And incline the ear of your heart!* As Fr. Deiss used to tell me, "Your heart is the primary preacher." The Word spoken to your ear has to match the Word that's already planted in the heart. So we need to listen

---

[5] Cf. Ps 95:7b–8a.

from the heart where we have pondered these things in our contemplation and our study, and "from the intimate sense of spiritual realities" that we ourselves have experienced. We have to listen from the deepest part of us, the ears of our hearts, from that I AM. And we need to speak from there too, but of course we can only do that after we have found that place in us—and it may take a lot of cleaning out to do so, but that's another story. We need to listen and speak from that heart, from that I AM planted deep within us, because then we will speak with authority, with the authority that God grants through Jesus.

This is not to deny the authority of the Church over interpretation of Scripture, since it is the Church that wrote the Scriptures, the Church that was the birthplace of the Scriptures (that's one of the reasons we refer to liturgy as "primary theology"; the Scriptures were written to be read there), and it was the Church that decided which books were authentic and canonical. But it does ask us to wonder who "the Church" is? You could say that the Church really begins with Mary *pondering these things in her heart* and *'blessed are all who hear the Word of God and keep it.'*[6]

∽

With all that in mind hear again this story of the exchange between Jesus and a scribe in Mark 12.

> One of the scribes came near and heard them disputing with one another, and seeing that Jesus answered them well, he asked him, "Which commandment is the first of all?" Jesus answered, "The first is, 'Hear, O Israel: the Lord

---

[6] Lk 2:19; 11:28.

our God, the Lord is one; you shall love the Lord your God with all your heart, and with all your soul, and with all your mind, and with all your strength.' The second is this, 'You shall love your neighbor as yourself.' There is no other commandment greater than these." Then the scribe said to him, "You are right, Teacher; you have truly said that 'he is one, and besides him there is no other'; and 'to love him with all the heart, and with all the understanding, and with all the strength,' and 'to love one's neighbor as oneself'—this is much more important than all whole burnt-offerings and sacrifices." When Jesus saw that he answered wisely, he said to him, "You are not far from the kingdom of God." After that no one dared to ask him any question.[7]

What is so unusual about this story is that this guy at first glance is simply parroting back to Jesus what Jesus had just said. I can imagine the other folks around them, including the apostles who always seem to be missing the point, especially in the Gospel of Mark, scratching their heads saying, "Hey, what'd he do? How come Jesus says he's so close to the kingdom? He never said that to me!" But somehow Jesus knew that this fellow wasn't just giving him empty words, undigested glop or pious claptrap.

This incident reminds me of another story from the Buddhist tradition about what is called the first "dharma transmission," when the Buddha wanted to pick a successor for himself before he died. The Zen tradition maintains that when the Buddha wanted to transmit his awakening,[8] he

---

[7] Mk 12:28–34.

[8] The Pali tradition tells the story of the Buddha passing on his teaching to his disciples immediately after his enlightenment instead.

gathered his monks together and instead of offering them a spoken teaching he simply held up a flower and remained silent. Those gathered were rather perplexed by that. But one of his disciples, named Mahakasyapa, smiled. And he was the one to be the successor.

How to explain this? It's perhaps foolish to try, but let me take a humble stab. In both cases it's as if both the scribe and Mahakasyapa—as well as the young monk in the "one-finger Zen" story in his pain—were totally present to the present moment, so there could be a direct transmission, mind to mind, heart to heart. It's as if the wind came along and blew the clouds away to reveal the moon. Nothing got in the way of the direct message or obscured the whole of what the other was conveying. The disciple Mahakasyapa was able to intuitively enter into that same reality with the Buddha in that moment, and so he smiled in understanding. The scribe in the story merely repeated back to Jesus what Jesus had already said, but somehow Jesus knew that he was not just parroting the words back, but was actually speaking them from a place of understanding and ownership. No filter, no nuance, no hidden meanings.

We've probably all had those moments when we feel like we have been saying the same thing over and over again, and people listen, and they nod knowingly, maybe even patronizingly, but we get the sense that they haven't really heard a word we've said. Well, Jesus too might have been teaching the same message over and over again in his itinerant preaching ministry, and people may have been either walking away stunned or saying, "Yes, Master. Whatever you say, Master." But this guy gets it. Finally Jesus was hearing something more than empty words in response. I try to imagine this scribe and Jesus looking each other dead-on in the eyes, and imagine the thrill in this guy's heart, the rush of energy through his veins when he hears, "You are not far from the reign of God."

Actually, though, this scribe does add one little phrase to what Jesus said, and it might be that phrase that really got Jesus' attention and let Jesus know that this guy knew what he was talking about—that this loving of God and neighbor was *'more important than all burnt offerings and sacrifices.'* This is not an uncommon theme in the Jewish Scriptures, from the prophet Isaiah to the psalms, and it seems to have been a favorite theme of Jesus himself, an echo of a line from Hosea 6 that Matthew puts on the lips of Jesus twice in his gospel: *It is love that I desire, not sacrifice, knowledge of God rather than holocaust.*[9] The sacrificial offerings can be nothing more than fire insurance, the appeasing of an idol. The theme that runs through the prophet Hosea, the reason Hosea was asked to marry Gomer, who went off and gave herself to prostitution, is to remind Israel that this covenant is a marriage, a relationship that they had been cheating on, and not just a magic formula. And so Jesus is inviting his listeners and us to be in relationship with God, with his Abba, not to simply appease God with any kind of sacrifice. And the same goes for our relationship with one another: We don't just play nice and act justly so that we don't go to hell—it's all about relationship. *The second is this, "You shall love your neighbor as yourself."* Part and parcel of our relationship with God, according to Jesus, is actually entering into relationship with one another, with all of the bumps and bruises and missteps and messiness that entails.

And "love," as you know, is one of the emptiest words going around, maybe it always has been. My experience in Asia is that folks think we Americans say "thank you" and "I love you" so much they have become devoid of meaning. I

---

[9] Hos 6:6; Mt 9:13, 12:7.

remember a young Chinese guy who had just immigrated to the States telling me once years ago that he could not believe how often people used the word "love" in America. He said something like, "Oh, we never use the word love until we are ready to settle down and marry someone and stay with them forever." To love somebody really meant something. I do not advocate saying "thank you" and "I love you" less, necessarily, but I do think we should really think of the weight of those words whenever we say them.

When the scribe adds on this little mention of how this love is more important than "sacrifice," I take that to symbolize outer observances in general. All our rules and habits and customs can actually be ways of avoiding God, keeping God at bay out of fear by obeying the rules without ever really having a relationship, like a parent that gives money instead of attention and love, or a spouse that goes through the motions of remembering an anniversary or spending "quality time." Empty gestures to join the empty words. We can do all the right things in a relationship and never really be present. Perfunctory observance, following objective standards, in some cases is still better than nothing, both in our relationship with God and in our relationships with others. But at some point in our life, we need to make the leap of being really present to all of those relationships, our relationship to God and our relationship to others, but quite often that only occurs when we begin to be really present to ourselves through the path of self-knowledge. (And that too is part of a whole other story.)

☙

Back to preaching: one more anecdote. There's a story told about an old priest who came to fill in at a parish. Everyone thought he was a kindly old man, a grandfather type. The first Sunday he got up to preach and he said simply, "Beloved, let us love God with all our hearts, and with all our soul, and with all our minds, and with all our strength, and let's love one another as Christ loved us." And then he sat down. Well, the people thought that was charming and everyone commented on what a fine preacher he was. It wasn't what the gospel of the day was about, but it didn't matter. Always a timely topic, and he didn't waste words, got right to the point—and got them out of church on time too!

The second week comes along, and he finishes reading the gospel, everyone sits down and he says, "Beloved, let us love God with all our hearts, and with all our soul, and with all our minds, and with all our strength, and let's love one another as Christ loved us." And he sat down. Well, the people looked at each other embarrassedly, thinking maybe their new priest was already in some form of senility and didn't remember that he had just said that last week. But everyone got out of Mass on time, and they forgot about it.

But the next week the very same thing happened: "Beloved, let us love God with all our hearts, and with all our soul, and with all our minds, and with all our strength, and let's love one another as Christ loved us." This time there was a wave of murmuring throughout the church, and maybe a little irritation. "What kind of trick is the diocese trying to pull on us by sending us this doddery old guy who keeps saying the same thing over and over again?!" And sure enough it happened again the fourth Sunday. This time the pillars of the parish gathered around old Ellen, who was the head of the parish council and a long-standing member of the church, and they deputized her to go and address this with Father. So she did, as politely but sternly as possible, saying, "Excuse me, Father, but we are all a little confused. This is your fourth week with us, and you have preached the exact same sermon every time."

"Do you remember what it was?" he asked in response, with a clarity that she was not expecting. "Yes, you said, 'Beloved, let us love God with all our hearts, and with all our soul, and with all our minds, and with all our strength, and let's love one another as Christ loved us.'" "That's right!" he said looking her dead in the eye. "I see you have heard, but I'm not sure anyone has really listened yet. So I'm going to keep on saying the same thing every week until I see someone start doing it."

☙

Now, let's bring it home.

It may seem like a bit of a pivot to start out talking about authority and end up talking about love, but as far as I can tell in the gospel of Jesus that's where real authority comes from—Jesus' relationship with his abba and Jesus' love especially for the sheep without a shepherd, the poor, the lepers, the outcasts, the tax collectors, and prostitutes. And he tells us, and the scribe here echoes it, that for us too it's all about love, the perfect love that casts out all fear, the love that is more important than ritual sacrifice, and the greatest love of all that washes feet and lays its life down for its friends. If we have decided that we want what Jesus had and are willing to go to any lengths to get it, then we will commit ourselves to loving God with all our hearts, all our soul, all our minds, and all our strength, and loving our neighbor—even our enemy!—as we love our own selves. Without that, as Saint Paul understood, we are just noisy gongs or clanging cymbals, even if we are saying so-called religious words. Who we are speaks much louder than anything we're saying. We only have the authority to cast out demons, forgive sins, and announce the Good News if and when those things are rooted in love of God and love for our neighbor.

Apparently, this is where Fr. Bede's authority came from. Toward the end of his life he wrote, "What is the meaning of life? The meaning of life is to love and there are two ways to love. One is through a dedication of the whole of your life to the spirit and the working out of that dedication. The other is to love another human being so profoundly that that initiates you into the divine love."

Speaking of pious claptrap, the phrase "Christian values" has become a kind of buzzword (if not an out-and-out dog whistle) in the American political realm, and it always leaves me wondering what exactly those Christian values are that are being referred to. Listening to the political discourse and how this term gets bandied about, you'd think it mainly meant protection of the traditional nuclear family and fighting against all the concomitant issues around sexuality—abortion, gay marriage, transgender rights, and so on. Honestly, at times it seems like "the right to bear arms" gets thrown in there too as a Christian value. A US congresswoman once referred to the death of Jesus in a joke about gun rights at a Christian event, hinting that Jesus may have prevented his crucifixion if he owned an AR-15 assault weapon.

I was involved in a discussion about the political realm once, a discussion that left me quite shaken because it ended up so far to the so-called "right" of the spectrum, and during the discussion that phrase got brought up several times. I went to bed that evening really wrestling with it, wanting to articulate my own belief. What I came up with was the seven corporal works of mercy, based on Matthew 25. To me these are authentic Christian values: feed the hungry, give drink to the thirsty, clothe the naked, give shelter to travelers, visit the sick, visit the imprisoned, and bury the dead. And one more thing, that I think is the reason I love and always have loved the Gospel of Jesus, and if I have any pastoral instincts as an ordained minister of the Church, it is based on this: radical inclusivity. Nobody gets left out, everyone gets brought to their dignity, everybody gets a second (and a third and a fourth chance, seventy times seven), even my enemy.

But then, I will admit, I did an internet search to find out what is commonly considered to be the list of Christian values, and I was pleasantly shocked by what came up. The first list was "love, humility, kindness, peace, respect, generosity, and forgiveness." Other listings for core Christian values were simply the fruits of the Spirit (Galatians 5:22–26): love, joy, peace, forbearance, kindness, goodness, faithfulness, gentleness, and self-control. Others of course mention belief in God along with "living a moral life and practicing what you preach." But the answer that really resonated with me came from a place called the Oak CE Learning Foundation, which summed it all up with one word: love. "Love is the core Christian value for our schools, because in the Bible we learn that God is Love and that God showed how much he loves us and how to love others." Ah . . .

Is this what people mean when they use the phrase "Christian values"? I suggest we challenge them on it, to make sure it's not just empty words, undigested glop, or pious claptrap. I'd love to hear someone read Galatians 5:22–26 on the fruits of the Spirit from the floor of the House or Senate. "My esteemed colleagues, I simply want to ensure that this bill is rooted in the Christian values that this country was founded on—joy, peace, forbearance, kindness, goodness, faithfulness, gentleness, self-control, and most of all love. With that I yield my time . . ."

I can't imagine how any person of goodwill of any tradition could disagree with these values.

One of the most hopeful things to happen in the world of interreligious dialogue in the last decades started out with an unfortunate misunderstanding. Pope Benedict XVI gave a lecture at the University of Regensburg on September 12, 2006, on the subject of faith and reason. It focused mainly on Christianity and what Pope Benedict called the tendency in the modern world to "exclude the question of God" from reason. Islam also features in a part of the lecture. For some reason, the pope quoted a Byzantine Emperor's strong criticism of Muhammad's teachings. Pope Benedict clarified that this was not his own personal opinion and described the quotation as being of a "startling brusqueness . . . which leaves us astounded." Throughout the world, however, a lot of people thought it was very insensitive of him to use the quote at all. And of course, many Muslims were very offended.

But one month later 38 Islamic scholars, representing all branches of Islam, replied to the pope in a very polite letter, titled "An Open Letter to the Pope," clarifying some teachings about Islam. And then a year later, 138 Islamic personalities co-signed another open letter, titled "A Common Word between Us and You," aimed at promoting interfaith dialogue. They title itself comes from Surah 3:64 of the Qur'an when Allah says to the prophet, "Say: O People of the Book! Let us come to a common word between us and you." They start out by quoting two other surahs of the Qur'an, 112 and 73, that speak of the necessity of loving God, and a *hadith* (a saying) of the Prophet Muhammad that exhorts love of neighbor. They then compare that to Jesus' two greatest commandments in the Gospel of Mark. And they conclude

> Thus in obedience to the Holy Qur'an, we as Muslims invite Christians to come together with us on the basis of what is common to us, which is also what is most

essential to our faith and practice: the Two Commandments of love.

What is not mentioned here, but I always highlight when I teach about this, is that Jesus is quoting the Jewish Scriptures (Deuteronomy 6:4 and Leviticus 19:18, 34), so all three of the People of the Book are present in this exhortation.

Let's keep it simple: this is something we hold in common among our traditions. It's all about love.

Someday we're going to realize that—that it's all about having our hearts of stone turned into hearts of flesh, that it's all about being in right relationship with God and with one another, and that the rest, as the great Jewish rabbis say, is just commentary. And the clouds will part, and the sun will shine through and everything else will fall into place. We'll finally understand the heart of the Gospel of Jesus. And we'll start to speak—and listen—with real authority.

And we'll suddenly, maybe sadly, realize that everything else has just been pious claptrap, empty words, and undigested glop.

Conclusion

On Meditating the Scriptures

Bede Griffiths used to use the word "meditate" (in the *lectio* sense, as we have discussed at the beginning, to ruminate over something) in a very interesting way. He would leave out the preposition and speak not of meditating *on* the Scriptures, but "meditating the Scriptures" and "meditating sacred texts from other traditions." There is an immediacy to this usage of the verb that I really like.

The four stages of the ancient monastic practice of *lectio divina* are reading (*lectio*), meditation (*meditatio*, in the sense we have been speaking of here), prayer (*oratio*), and then contemplation (*contemplatio*). I have suggested that that final step, contemplation, is the equivalent of silent meditation in the Asian sense, coming to one-pointed concentration, perhaps even using a small morsel of the Scripture reading itself as a type of mantra to lead us into the silence from which it came. These four readings are meant to take us deeper into our own consciousness and let the Word and Wisdom speak to us there and unfold its deeper meanings.

Certainly, every text has some kind of literal meaning, and so we try to understand the historical context, and translate it from an ancient mentality into our own. That is a good start, but hermeneutics and exegesis cannot necessarily reveal meaning.

In addition to the literal meaning there are the symbolic meanings of Scripture—the ethical and allegorical meanings, as well as a spiritual, mystical meaning. There is an ancient teaching about this that seems to have originated with the storied second- to third-century exegete Origen of Alexandria. He taught that just as the human person is body, soul, and spirit, so there is a literal, moral, and spiritual meaning, which are the somatic, psychic, and spiritual meanings of Scripture. He compares Scripture to an almond: the literal meaning is just the bitter rind, and if you try to reduce the divine meaning to the purely external significance of the words, "the Word will return to its secret dwelling." If we ruminate further, we might learn the ethical meaning, which Origen said was the Word's protective shell, but that requires a course of careful purification. This is a reference to what the ancient monastic tradition called compunction, the heart being pierced with sorrow for sin, leading to repentance and forgiveness. As Olivier Clement wrote, "The meaning is revealed only to prayer, and certainly to prayer with tears." Only then might the spiritual kernel be reached, which Origen thought was what really mattered, that which feeds the soul on the mysteries of divine wisdom.

This way of approaching Scripture could also be applied to reading texts from other spiritual traditions as well. Reading non-Christians texts is not an uncommon practice among what is known as the Christian Ashram movement in India, at the beginning of or even during the liturgy. (The latter was never officially sanctioned by the Church.) India, of course, is a spiritual environment that easily lends itself to acknowledging the "seeds of the Word" (the famous phrase of the second-century St. Justin Martyr) that are already present in other revelations.

Not just studying sacred texts from other traditions, but actually meditating them for my personal *lectio*, has been a regular personal practice of mine since very early on in monastic life, particularly after my first trips to our ashram Shantivanam in South India, where I first experienced the practice in person. I know that there is always a danger of what the late Jesuit William Harmless (in his excellent book *Mystics*) referred to as "cherry picking," lining up isolated phrases that happen to share a common word or a turn of a phrase and saying, "You see: it's all the same!" This is not at all what I mean. I mean a deep reading, knowing something of the context and the culture that gave birth to the literature as well as discovering the levels of meaning in the text itself. Bede's deep reading of the Bhagavad Gita led him to write an entire commentary on it (a book titled *The River of Compassion*), and Abhishiktananda's meditation on the Upanishads produced an introduction to them that made up the second part of one of his best-known books, *The Further Shore*. William Harmless himself in that same book *Mystics* did a masterly job of dissecting the writings of both the thirteenth-century Japanese Zen master Dogen and the great Persian mystic poet Rumi of the same century.

This can be done with the aim of understanding that other tradition, of course, but it can also be done to get a new view of our own tradition. Part of becoming a world church is being able to express Christianity in new language, which may mean expanding beyond our Greco-Roman Eurocentric philosophy and mind-set. This might be done with an evangelical aim in mind, to bring the Gospel to new lands and peoples. As Raimundo Panikkar put it, "If Christ is to have any meaning for Hindus, Andines, Ibos, Vietnamese, and others who do not belong to the Abrahamic lineage, this meaning can no longer be offered in the garb of Western philosophies."

However, and more immediately, it can lead me, the reader, to a new depth in understanding my own tradition, aspects that I might never have noticed. William Johnson wrote beautifully and often about how certain Asian traditions and the Asian approach to mysticism in general can reveal new aspects of the Gospel to Western Christians, aspects that have been there all along but that we simply haven't noticed. And these other ways might be able to help us understand the depth of our own kerygma and traditions, as well as help us find a new vocabulary to understand and express Jesus' experience for ourselves and to a new age. Or as the late theologian Ewert Cousins explained, often the partners in dialogue with another tradition discover in that other tradition "values which are submerged or only inchoate in their own."

Obviously, though I have limited myself here to a dialogue between a Western European mind-set with some of the traditions of Asia, this approach does not only apply to Asian spirituality. My elder confrere Bruno Barnhart wrote beautifully (in his introduction to a chapter titled "The Eternal Religion" in a collation of Bede Griffiths's writings called *The One Light*) that not only is the Mystery present in a different way in other traditions, but we are to learn from all of them, "from the primal, tribal religions as well as the highly developed traditions of Hinduism and Christianity." Furthermore, he says, the only reason that external religion exists with its rites, dogmas, and institutional structures, is "to bring people to the personal experience of this mystery." Toward that end, all external forms, all the language of religion, has to be continually revised if it is to communicate the mystery to people of a new age. At the same time—and this is equally vital—the mystery actually "already dwells in the heart of every human being, and the church must awaken to this 'universal revelation.'" Grace builds on nature.

What thinkers such as Fr. Bede and Abhishiktananda asked was, instead of or in addition to Greco-Roman thought, what if Christianity could be interpreted and passed on using the language of the Vedanta (late Indian philosophy, based on the Upanishads), the language of Mahayana Buddhism, or the language of Taoist philosophy? And even if that wasn't done in the past, why cannot it not be done now? Is it possible to take our experience of the Gospel and our tradition, and try to articulate them using other philosophical or mystical language? Bede and Abhishiktananda thought that the failure of missionary efforts in Asia, especially in India, might have come from using a philosophical language that makes little sense to the Asian mind. We have so often tried to pass on Greek terms and Roman culture—hence Plato and Aristotle, the Roman Rite of the Mass, and Gregorian chant—instead of allowing the seed of the kerygma to take root in the soil of native philosophical and cultural genius, allowing that the spark of the Divine, the inspiration of the Holy Spirit, has been at work in other traditions as well.

Who agreed with this was none other than Pope Saint John Paul II. In a 1998 encyclical titled *Fides et Ratio* (#72) the Holy Father acknowledges that Christianity first encountered Greek philosophy in preaching the Gospel. But he says that this does not mean that other approaches are excluded. As the Gospel comes into contact with cultural worlds which have been outside of Christian influence, this is part of the task of inculturation, to be open to other philosophical approaches. And he said, "My thoughts turn immediately to the lands of the East, so rich in religious and philosophical traditions of great antiquity." And then he added, "Among these lands, India has a special place."

Is it absolutely necessary for everyone to engage in such a practice? No. But to those like me who have the thirst, it has been of inestimable value. All of the exploration of the other spiritual traditions has only made me fall in love with Jesus even more, and I feel more dedicated to the Gospel than ever.

For those interested in further exploration of the texts I have referred to here, these are some recommendations of translations and versions that have served me well. As the Italians say, *Tradurre è tradire*—"To translate is to betray." So we must always recognize that unless we are reading any sacred text in its original language, we are most likely not getting much of the subtlety of the cultural mind-set, and that includes the Jewish Scriptures in Hebrew as well as the New Testament in Greek, of course. That ought not dissuade us, only keep us humble.

For scholarly translations of the Upanishads, I rely on Patrick Olivelle and Valerie Roebuck, but I also have a dog-eared copy of a version prepared in the 1940s by Swami Prabhavananda with Frederick Manchester titled *Breath of the Eternal* that I have carried with me for years. It is not an exact translation, but it is very readable and very accessible. I also have a well-worn copy of the Bhagavad Gita that was prepared by Swami Nikhilananda that was bought for me by a *parivrajaka* ("wandering monk") I met on the banks of the Ganges in North India, the most Christ-like person I have ever encountered. The Tao te Ching is one of the most translated texts in history (after the Bible, *Le Petit Prince*, and *The Adventures of Pinocchio*). I was first introduced to it in the popular Gia-fu Feng/Jane English translation with its luxurious black-and-white photographs, which has now been updated. But my favorite version for years has been the one prepared by the late American poet Sam Hamill. A good introduction to Chuang-tzu would be Thomas Merton's *The Way of Chuang Tzu*. Of the two Buddhist texts I mentioned in the introduction, I cherish the translation of the Dhammapada done by Ananda Maitreya issued by Parallax Press with a foreword by Thich Nhat Hanh, and the popular teacher Pema Chödrön's commentary on Shantideva's *Guide to the Bodhisattva's Way of Life* called *No Time to Lose*.

For the writings of Bede Griffiths, outside of his classic autobiography *The Golden String*, which charts his life up until his departure for India, his most popular book is *Return to the Center*, which I have been told he recommended to people as well as an introduction to his thought. I am pleased to say that Orbis Books issued a new version of it since it had gone out of print, for which I myself wrote a long biographical introduction. Abhishiktananda's books have mostly also passed out of print, but a beautiful, updated version of *Swami Abhishiktananda: His Life Told through His Letters* was released in 2025. Orbis Books also did a collection of each of their writings in their Modern Spiritual Masters series. I also have recommended William Johnson's *Arise My Love: Mysticism for a New Era* to anyone who would listen.

Let me end by repeating and expanding on the words of my beloved late confrere and mentor Bruno Barnhart, whom I cited above. I believe that the Mystery of the Divine is present in a unique way in every authentic spiritual tradition. And we can learn from them all, from the primal, tribal religions all the way through to highly developed traditions such as Hinduism, Buddhism, and Taoism with their great philosophical schools and ritual life. But if we really want to know this Mystery, we need to penetrate, as Bruno says, "through the exterior shell of the rationalized system" and realize within ourselves the original experience: that is, "participate in the divine life which has been shared among human beings." This is the real Reign of God and the essential message of all religion, my version of what I have called the *telos*. Bruno continues by saying that external religion, with its rites, dogmas, and institutional structures, only exists—and this is one of those "onlys" that you could say over and over again: external religion only, only, only exists to bring people to a personal experience of this mystery. And so the external forms of religion and its language need to be continually revised to be able to communicate this mystery to the people of a new age. That is what I have been attempting to do in my work and in these pages.

The mystery, however, already dwells in your heart—and in the heart of every human being. What an epiphany that is!

Acknowledgments

Special thanks to Robert Ellsberg and Orbis Books for their vote of confidence on this second book for them; to oblates Lisa Benner and Matt Fisher, and fellow writer Stephen Copeland, who encouraged this project; to Bob Peck for not only providing me the beloved anchorage from which I wrote the first of these meditations, but who also served as eagle-eyed editor; to all the luminous souls around the world who hosted me during my sabbatical year, of which this work was the unexpected fruit.